# N.C. WYETH

**SELF PORTRAIT** (1913)
Oil on canvas, h:18¼, w:12¼
Unsigned
Courtesy of Mr. & Mrs. Nicholas Wyeth

# N.C. WYETH

## THE COLLECTED PAINTINGS,

## ILLUSTRATIONS & MURALS

**DOUGLAS ALLEN AND DOUGLAS ALLEN, JR.**

WITH A FOREWORD BY PAUL HORGAN

AND AN INTRODUCTION BY RICHARD LAYTON

WINGS BOOKS

NEW YORK • AVENEL, NEW JERSEY

Illustrations compilation copyright © 1972 by Douglas Allen and Douglas Allen, Jr.
Text 1972 by Douglas Allen and Douglas Allen, Jr.
All rights reserved under International and Pan-American Copyright Conventions.

No part of this book may be reproduced or transmitted in any form or by any means electronic or
mechanical including photocopying, recording, or by any information storage and retrieval system,
without permission in writing from the publisher.

This 1996 edition is published by Wings Books,
a division of Random House Value Publishing, Inc.,
40 Engelhard Avenue, Avenel, New Jersey 07001,
by arrangement with Crown Publishers, Inc.

Wings Books and colophon are trademarks of Random House Value Publishing, Inc.

Random House
New York • Toronto • London • Sydney • Auckland
http://www.randomhouse.com/

Printed and bound in China

**Library of Congress Cataloging-in-Publication Data**

Wyeth, N.C. (Newell Convers), 1882-1945
    N.C. Wyeth : the collected paintings, illustrations, and murals /
  by Douglas Allen and Douglas Allen, Jr. ; with a foreword by Paul
  Horgan and an introduction by Richard Layton.
        p.   cm.
    Includes index.
    ISBN 0-517-18335-8
    1. Wyeth, N. C. (Newell Convers), 1882–1945—Themes, motives.
  2. Wyeth, N. C. (Newell Convers), 1882–1945—Bibliography.
  I. Allen, Douglas.  II. Allen, Douglas 1935–       III. Title.
  ND237.W94A4  1996
  759.13—dc20                                          96–15721
                                                          CIP

15 14 13 12 11 10 9 8 7 6

DESIGNED BY GEORGE HORNBY

$T$HIS BOOK IS DEDICATED to the memory of two departed friends—the late Helen L. Card and E. Walter Latendorf. They devoted themselves to the advancement of American illustration as a great art. Their like will not be seen again.

ROMANCE OF ADVENTURE
National Association of Book Publishers poster
for Children's Book Week © 1928

# Contents

Preface    9

Foreword    11

Introduction    15

1. Howard Pyle's World of Illustration    19
2. Wyeth's Student Years    22
3. N.C.'s West    33
4. The Indian in His Solitude    57
5. Brandywine Country    63
6. Religious Painting    73
7. The Classics    79
8. From Blackbeard to St. Nick    123
9. Commercial Art    141
10. Murals, Lunettes, and the Triptych    157
11. Easel Painting    173

With Gratitude    193

Notes    195

Index    197

# Preface

THERE WERE three basic reasons for my attempting a book on N.C. Wyeth.

The first was my long-standing interest in the works of that large group of artists who devoted their lives to making the pictures that, reproduced on the printed pages of books and magazines, have given such great pleasure to countless people over the years.

The second was my admiration for N.C. Wyeth, not only as an artist but as a man. He was deeply dedicated to his profession, his home, his friends, and especially to his family, a family that has carried on in his tradition, thereby tendering him a greater memorial than monuments, plaques, or even mere words.

The third reason was more personal. It is a part of my own life. Some twenty or more years have passed since I was suddenly exposed to the art of N. C. Wyeth under somewhat different circumstances. Previously I had known of his work only through his brilliant illustrations for the Scribner Illustrated Classics, that library of great books especially selected as outstanding literature for young people. In those days, my special hobby was—it still is—the great artists who portrayed the Old West: in particular, Frederic Remington. In my frequent trips to bookshops specializing in the old and rare, in search of new finds to add to my own collection, I was at times accompanied by a young boy, who delighted in the browsing and rummaging as much as I did. One of these outings resulted in his discovering a copy of the limited edition of James Boyd's *Drums*, a Scribner Illustrated Classic, signed both by the author and by the illustrator, N.C. Wyeth.

Buying that book was my undoing. From that time on, there had to be other trips for other books and other periodicals and other prints—my young son's Wyeth collection became bigger and bigger. My own dream of someday owning an original Remington went aglimmer as they became ever scarcer and more costly.

The young boy has grown to manhood now, and his N.C. Wyeth collection has grown with him. And, as the years passed, I too developed a constantly increasing appreciation for the magnificent contribution N. C. Wyeth had made to the field of American illustration and art.

One fine day the inevitable happened. We discussed doing a book on N.C. Wyeth. The idea had considerable appeal. However, the little I knew about him and his work had been picked up casually through friends who dealt in books and art—it was hardly enough on which to base a comprehensive presentation. There followed years of library research by both of us, innumerable visits to art galleries, and constant reference to my son's extensive collection—before we came to this: our book on N. C. Wyeth and his art.

As I worked on the text, I realized that N. C. could speak best for himself in so many instances that I have quoted him freely. My son and I hope that our joint efforts to present a thorough, rounded view of N.C. Wyeth and his art will enable the reader to share our enthusiasm and admiration.

DOUGLAS ALLEN

LONG JOHN SILVER AND HAWKINS (*To me he was unweariedly kind; and always glad to see me in the galley.*)
Oil on canvas, h:48, w:40
Signed upper left: N. C. Wyeth
*Treasure Island,* by Robert Louis Stevenson
Charles Scribner's Sons, 1911
Courtesy of Mrs. Andrew Wyeth

# Foreword

## I

THIS is a lifetime we are looking at.

## II

N. C. Wyeth was most widely known as an illustrator. For years there poured forth from his workshop series after series of pictures dramatizing high moments out of classic tales for young people. Through the technique of color reproduction, these works reached an enormous public. They were all characterized by admirable draughtsmanship, pleasure in the dramatic range of human character, and above all, a powerful sense of mood. Wyeth was unique in the most distinctive quality of his story pictures, and that was a most beguiling sense of conviction. By the magic of his rich nature, he was able to imagine himself *there*, in whatever situation his author set forth. This gave him a delightful authority by which he transcended the disadvantages of never personally having been in Sherwood Forest, or at the Admiral Benbow Inn, or in that little Austrian town where the Angel Satan* came in the guise of a beautiful youth to play his melancholy role of detached observer of the woes of men and women.

It was a fine achievement to have educated with his fond and exciting images of storied life the imaginations of the children of his time. He played, really, an educational role in them, which was the expression of his conscience, and in it there are three fine values which moved him powerfully. The first of these was his love for America. He loved it for its landscape, its spiritual belief in the individual human being, and for any separate expression of that belief, however (and even especially) original or outlandish it might be. The second of the values which moved him as he re-created the past was his joy in the trappings of historical period. He was an exhaustive student of historical periods, and loved accuracy of detail with a scholar's respect for the facts. Some accident of his taste made him especially effective in two periods, the medieval time and the American Colonial era. But to say this is not to depreciate his virtuosity in such affairs as giants, all kinds of ships, or the limning of the fabulous. The third of his moving values was his love for the beauty of humanity, the face, the form, and the attitude of man and woman.

* In *The Mysterious Stranger,* by Mark Twain.

And it is with that value that his work as illustrator merges into his work as a painter of freer subject matter. For he drew incessantly, at the proper study of mankind. The largeness of spirit visible in even his less important illustrations called for a larger expression than their subject matter sometimes might suggest. He painted many murals, some on an heroic scale. Like most of the murals in the world including the very greatest, they were larger illustrations than those found in the pages of a book. This is not to confuse or interchange the way murals and book illustrations are conceived. It is only to say that it is historically absurd to exclude a painter who is a first class illustrator from the company of more serious or abstract painters on the grounds that he is merely an illustrator. It is essentially an illustrative function to arrest in painting a great episode in spiritual or political history for the celebration of the past and the inspiration of the future. Wyeth in his murals—most of them, so far as I know, painted on canvas and later applied to the wall—treated many moments of American history, and otherwise celebrated symbolically the course of human life. Such works are mentioned here primarily to compose the opposite points of view which are held about the dignity of the illustrator's role. What is relevant finally is just this: whether the illustrator is or is not a good artist. With the evidence increasing in every phase of his growth, up to the very last, it is clear through the range of his lifetime's work that Wyeth was indeed a very good artist and possibly a great one.

## III

It is interesting to speculate for a moment upon what formed the style of this painter. Even in its experimental phases it is a curiously consistent style, it has a signature in every line and reach of light that is unmistakably his. His color is rich, warm, and freshly harmonious. He has an extraordinary skill at capturing the quality of light itself, not merely its symbolic representation in the arrangement of planes and their shadows, and he exercised it to the fullest, with an almost offhand delight in his mastery. His compositions are massive, with the play of great bodies, or loom of rock, or rise of tree, or the bulk of something fashioned by builders. There is substance to his forms and reality to his objects.

And in the mood in which these components are brought together there is an unstated spiritual quality which sets us to thinking that with all his remarkable power and command of his craft, he was always, even in his least serious work, seeking to say more than could meet the eye.

That, indeed, is the grand element in his personal style. It is what spoke to the countless youth in his paintings of mood and action, and it is what he triumphantly realized in his last, most personal works—that power of both representing and commenting upon human life which has always been to their varying degrees the characteristic of true artists in all media.

Because his style has two major aspects, we will look in perhaps contrasting directions to find their origins.

When he was a very young man, Wyeth spent a year or so in the American Southwest. I feel this experience had much to do with how he ever afterward saw Nature. He saw it there, under the sun which so vastly plays light upon mountains, and plains, and continents of clouds, in a grand abstraction. That light and that landscape became his symbols for fabled places when later he needed to represent them.

His apprenticeship as a painter was served in Wilmington and Chadds Ford under Howard Pyle whose powerful personality drew a whole school of American illustrators to him. Pyle's vision of romance and dramatic composition marked Wyeth's development very plainly. We see Pyle now as a period artist, with respect for his fine craftsmanship, and with the extent of his growth historically plain. Nearer to Wyeth, we see in him a far greater range than Pyle commanded, even as we acknowledge the younger man's debt to the older.

Philosophically, Wyeth drew much of his sense of people from the faith of the New England transcendentalists. He was a New Englander all his life, of the temper of Emerson and Thoreau. When he idealized his human subjects, they often came out with the calm of a rather bleak faith in their faces, a Sunday afternoon excellence which undoubtedly was nearer to the American experience than the baroque conceits of the European masters. Among these masters, on the other hand, he revered Michelangelo above everyone else; and it is paying tribute in both directions to note that there is evidence of that respect in Wyeth's heroic handling of the figure in many of his works.

The affirmative, the optimistic flavor proper to the illustrative works is drawn, then, from the inexhaustible sunlight of the Southwest, from the studio experience under Pyle, and from the faith of the New England tradition. But there is another view to be had of experience and the likeness of life if we follow Wyeth's eye as he searches for expression which will unlock that which is not visible, and reveal the great theme of life under God. And here we find him in the company of those artists who, like Beethoven, spend themselves in the holy task of trying to release such beauty, form, and affirmation as dwell in the commonplace and the familiar, and give them noble substance worthy of their Creator. He avowed no religion altogether, though the dignity and plainness of the Quaker beliefs spoke to him. But his intensity of emotion and the respect he gave to the accessible world had much religious character, which meant endless search for two truths—his own, and Nature's.

No less a motive than that empowered Wyeth to grow and grow, in his last paintings, until his technical mastery came to serve rather than dominate; and his lifelong love of the human condition yielded him, and us, the fulfillment of its quest.

## IV

They are paintings of the American places and people he knew best . . . the Pennsylvania countryside and the Maine coast. They are painted in a technique which he undertook relatively late in his life: egg tempera on gesso panels, where heretofore he had worked in oil on canvas. In tempera, he found a new clarity and crispness. Its lucidity, and the quality of the plasterlike surface of gesso, had much to do with the sudden release of a vein of his thought and feeling long recognized but not delivered. With his familiar expertness, he mastered expression in the technique new to him and applied it both to illustrative work and to the more personal painting of his last few years.

In those paintings there is a contemplative mood which somehow carries the thought beyond the immediate subject matter. Their sombre lyricism is perhaps the truest echo of Wyeth's personality to be found in all his work. They give rise to such feeling and thought as we look at them that we are moved to say, while regarding his image of the world, "Here is what a man of very large nature had to say as he followed his task of celebrating and praising life through art: in every object or person there is beauty to be discovered, though now it prove to be tragic, or again innocent and hopeful; but in all things there is dignity, and it is my task that I find it, and set forth my view of life in such a way that those who look on what I have done will know that harmony I have sought to find between God's inscrutable designs and our daily course on earth; and all this with all my strength, my conscience and my spirit."

In so daring to paraphrase an artist's credo, I have here the advantage of long intimate years of friendship with Wyeth, and have heard his words on the subject. Yet I do not rely too heavily on that rich experience to make the conclusion. The evidence is there in the late pictures. It is there in terms of the color, in the massiveness of the designs, in the enchantments of his technical devotion to every problem of surface and of form; and again and above all, it speaks from the temper of the works, grave, exalted, attentive and at times almost worshipful or rapturous, as in the *Summer Night;* or the *Island Funeral,* with its godlike view; or the *Spring House,* with its little poems of natural joy in leaf and stone and flower all miraculously drawn, and clustered around the central homely splendor of the gorgeous milk, symbol of sustenance, pouring from the pail like light itself.

He loved the moment, the place, the person so much that in a period of art whose fashion it was to paint abstractions of the ego, he spent himself at the job representing truly that which he loved, while he served respect for the values of abstraction through respect for the art of design and composition. Light itself, weather, the atmosphere and its myriad spells, these seem to live a captured life in his pictures; not just their symbols and conventional signs. It is an American light, off the coast of Maine, or over the mellow Brandywine whose every change of daily mood he knew from living there. This is a quality which one day will be regarded as equal in interest and significance, in discovering Wyeth's place in American art, as it was in appraising the values of the French Impressionists' rediscovery of the properties of light in the atmosphere.

## V

All his various activities as are represented in this collection of his lifetime's growth sprang from a superb vitality. He was a big man, with an heroic head. His face was massively modelled, deeply marked by the wonders and doubts of his inner experience. His eyes were brilliant, and the play of his expression had a flashing range, from the merriment and charm with which he talked with friends and charged the characters of his large family, to a profound earnestness, a tragic and powerful look which could make a trivial topic suddenly assume a new and enlightening importance. His conversation was energizing. He was wonderfully articulate, playing through a vocabulary which had as many rich and colorful and striking notes as his palette. The variety of his work was honestly come by, for his personality, his mind, his interests, had countless aspects, all of them of that sort of versatility which reinforces rather than contradicts the central character of the man. He embodied goodness and generosity, tolerance and respect and encouragement, love for the simplest humanity of man, and impatience with nonsense or self-indulgence, and he worshipped the best he saw in Nature, humanity, and art.

Life was profuse wherever he made himself felt, and seemed better than it was, and more worthy of hard work and deserving of joy. He took great draughts of comfort and confirmation from music and literature as well as from the mightiest of his predecessors in the world of painting. He challenged his own spirit with the power and the compassion which he found in Beethoven, Michelangelo, and Shakespeare. As I have noted elsewhere,* Wyeth was quick to recognize and

* *Encounters With Stravinsky*, pp. 62 ff.

proclaim the true masters of new styles in his own century—such artists in music as Igor Stravinsky and Alban Berg, for example. A work he often had reference to was *The Dynasts*, by Thomas Hardy. He found in its godlike view and melancholy courage some grand statement of his own character. And on the other hand, he was ribald and hilarious among his family and friends. At the head of his table, he was a master of bounty, surrounded by children and grandchildren and friends and neighbors, with dogs under the chairs, and a profusion of foods on the board, and a riot of harmony in the air. Giving so much, he contained more than he could give.

It was, among other things, what made him so magnetic and powerful a teacher. Not only a teacher of his own art, but of those responsibilities of spirit and action which life itself demands and does not always see fulfilled. He did teach many artists, notably his own son Andrew, his daughters Henriette and Carolyn, and his sons-in-law, Peter Hurd and John McCoy II. But there were others, and of them all he demanded imitation not of his work, but of his love of work; and to them all he gave his full sense of how all that there is of life can pertain to a single act of art.

In other words, he had greatness as a man, in which his powers as an artist were deeply and securely rooted, and by which they were ever refreshed.

## VI

As an illustrator, he was head and shoulders above his contemporaries.

As "pure" painter, he left a rich legacy of works which celebrate his own image of his country. When we see it as he saw it, we will see him more truly—for so by the interaction of a creative interpreter and the places and conditions of his life we come to know, from his particular spiritual and physical experience passionately recorded, the universal values that abide in those acts of art which live long after the mortal span of the artist himself. He will be rediscovered in terms which were for the most part denied him during his lifetime.

Until then, his country inherits his beautiful tributes to the earthly likeness of mankind as he knew it.

PAUL HORGAN

# Introduction

With pictures by N. C. Wyeth. These words, appearing on the covers and pages of scores of magazines and books, have served to quicken the hearts and raise the expectations of young readers for three generations. To all of us as parents, librarians, or students of history, the name N. C. Wyeth has stood as a hallmark of special merit. In very large measure, it was his hand that gave form to our earliest concepts of heroism and adventure.

During the "golden" years of illustration in America, from the mid-1870s through the first decades of this century, many capable and creative talents found their way into print. Fewer were the really great ones, such as Winslow Homer, Howard Pyle, or Frederic Remington. Certainly, Newell Convers Wyeth was one of the "greats." Through forty-two years of illustrating, from 1903 until his death in 1945, Wyeth created a large body of important and lasting works—nearly four thousand in all. We now have at hand a valuable and comprehensive record cataloguing the products of this remarkable career, a career well worth examining.

When N. C. Wyeth arrived at Wilmington, Delaware, in 1902, the Howard Pyle School of Art had already gained wide and enthusiastic acclaim in the two short years since its inception. Pyle soon found in his new pupil an enthusiasm for learning coupled with a youthful impatience to put that learning to practical use. In the master, Wyeth found a rare individual of uncommon understanding and noble ideals.

At the very heart of Pyle's teaching was his concept of "Mental Projection." It was through this means, potentially, that one might sense fully whatever needed portraying on canvas. "One must live in the picture," Pyle stressed. Later, in his own teaching, Wyeth was to convey the same idea with expressions such as, "Don't just paint a sleeve—become the arm!" Something of the difference in the personalities of the two men is perhaps suggested in those brief statements, as well as a hint at the qualities that might be anticipated in their works. In Pyle's art can be perceived a distillation of the intellect; Wyeth's, on the other hand, seems forged by inner blows of an emotional urge. We might look, for comparison, to the separate series of masterful illustrations each did for the rollicking tales of *Robin Hood*, and perhaps find there those individual qualities. Nevertheless, like his mentor, Wyeth loved accuracy and authenticity in recording historical fact, but never became pedantic or a slave to mere detail. He always placed spirit above clinical fact.

N. C. Wyeth joyfully embraced life's daily experiences with an exuberance that is unmistakable, as is revealed in his art. Even as a boy, he enjoyed the labors that exposed him to the forces of nature. "My brothers and I were brought up on a farm, and from the time I could walk I was conscripted into doing every conceivable chore that there was to do about the place. This early training gave me a vivid appreciation of the part the body plays in action. Now, when I paint a figure on horseback, a man plowing, or a woman buffeted by the wind, I have an acute bodily sense of the muscle-strain, the feel of the hickory handle, or the protective bend of head and squint of eye that each pose involves. After painting action scenes, I have ached for hours because of having put myself in the other fellow's shoes as I realized him on canvas."

Because of his intense concentration on working from the costumed figure during his student years and after, Wyeth rarely needed to use models in his later work. Instead, he used his own figure to work out the needed expression or stance. An example that clearly demonstrates this is in one of the illustrations for *Drums*, in which the story's main character, Johnny Fraser, is depicted standing "On the Sea Wall with John Paul Jones." There, back to us, is the figure of the artist himself!

When the occasion did require a model, the individual was most often a member of the artist's family. As the family expanded, the choice of age and subject type increased, providing a convenient pool of readily-available assistants. The smiling Priscilla portrayed in *The Courtship of Miles Standish* and the beautiful dark-haired heroine of *Vandemark's Folly* are one and the same model, the patient and cooperative Mrs. N. C. Wyeth. And the handsome young gallant striking the required poses for *Anthony Adverse* is son Andrew, who gained through such experiences much helpful insight, soon to be similarly employed in his own celebrated works.

As N. C. Wyeth's art gained national recognition, marked especially by the advent of the great *Treasure Island* series in 1911, and with the issuing of each succeeding title of the Scribner's Classics, it is not surprising that he frequently was called upon to present his personal views on art and his advice to young illustrators. This he did, as Pyle had done before him, with a deep sense of responsibility. Fortunately, he had developed the ability of expressing himself in words almost as vividly as in pictures. On one occasion he remarked, "To a great number, art is principally an escape from life (a very sterile pleasure indeed) and they fail la-

[ 15 ]

THE FLIGHT ACROSS THE LAKE
Oil on canvas, h:40, w:32
Signed lower right: N. C. Wyeth
*The Last of the Mohicans*, by James Fenimore Cooper
Copyright 1919 Charles Scribner's Sons;
renewal copyright 1947 Carolyn B. Wyeth
Courtesy of Mrs. Russell G. Colt

mentably to grasp the fact that the cultivation of life through the arts is a vital need to inspired living." In a writing directed to students, he advised, "The genuineness of the artist's work depends upon the genuineness of the artist's living. In other words, art is not what you do, it is what you are. We cannot in art produce a fraction more than what we are."

In all that he did, he evidenced a profound reverence for the simple, familiar, and common things and experiences, finding fresh inspiration in his daily contacts with all life around him.

With this almost mystical view, and having spent his boyhood near Concord, it is not surprising that as he matured he was drawn strongly to the writings of Thoreau. This devotion continued throughout the greater part of his life. "Thoreau's tremendous force to me as an artist," he wrote to a friend, "lies within his ability to boil up the little into the big! He demonstrates the fact that to elevate the little into the great is genius."

N. C. Wyeth's art was ever evolving. In scanning the scope and changing style of his works, from first to last it is nothing short of remarkable. The talent which in its youth gave us "The Indian in His Solitude" and the memorable images of Bill Bones and Blind Pew was the same expansive genius that later could forge onto canvas the "Battle of Wilson's Creek" and "Wallace's

Vision"—and later still—"Walden Revisited" and "Nightfall." The record of his career provides an exciting view of a magnificent performance.

Just as N. C. Wyeth was a vital force in illustration, illustration has been a major force in American art, contributing much of what can be identified as genuinely original or innovative in painting idioms. Its position no longer needs defending.

Illustration today, however, is languishing, pale in the shadow of the vitality imparted by Homer, Remington, Pyle, and Wyeth. It has either lost or deserted its public, a public sated with overexposure to glossy photographic images.

In the face of the current dissipation and the plight of publishing generally, it is perhaps a phenomenon worth noting that the Wyeth-illustrated classics are still being reissued through popular demand, and rare first editions are sought by an ever-increasing number of avid collectors.

Though N. C. Wyeth spent the major portion of his life painting in the Brandywine country he most loved, he has passed on to us a testament of steadfast devotion to the highest of ideals in his art. His works will stand the test of time.

RICHARD LAYTON
*Wilmington, Delaware*

# N.C. WYETH

Howard Pyle at his easel (1898)
Courtesy of the Delaware Art Museum

1

# *Howard Pyle's World of Illustration*

N̲o ATTEMPT can be made to write about Newell Convers Wyeth without mention of the man who gave so much of himself in molding the character and creative gifts of the many young people associated with him in those years often termed the Golden Age of American Illustration.

During this period that had known Frederic Remington, A. B. Frost, E. W. Kemble, Charles Dana Gibson, and many other notable illustrators, one man stood apart. That man was Howard Pyle, renowned artist, classic writer, and profound student. His accomplishments were great and varied, but small when compared to his unselfish dedication to the schooling and training of a group of young, enthusi-

astic, and talented budding artists who were destined to make a priceless contribution to American art for decades.

Howard Pyle was at his productive peak that October of 1894 when he agreed to give "A Course in Practical Illustration" at the Drexel Institute of Art, Science and Industry in Philadelphia. At the time he had more commitments than he could handle and was absorbed in ideas for future projects as well. Why, then, did he decide to devote precious and lucrative time to training young people in the field of art? There were a number of reasons.

Pyle was wholeheartedly dedicated to his profession. He had noted with concern that many an apparently gifted young man and

THE GIANT
Oil on canvas, h:72, w:60
Signed lower left: N. C. Wyeth 1923
Courtesy of the Westtown School, Westtown,
    Pennsylvania
The children (*from left*) are William Clothier Engle
    (in whose memory the mural was painted), Henriette
    Wyeth, Ann Wyeth, Andrew Wyeth, Nathaniel Wyeth,
    and Carolyn Wyeth.

woman made an artistic debut in a flame of brilliance that all too soon flickered and faded. He felt that this decline was basically due to a lack of sound training, for he firmly believed that talent alone, without the basics of an education in the field of illustration, could not bring success in that profession. The underlying fault, he thought, was that the art schools of that period believed in the routine of endless hours spent copying from the classic plaster cast and drawing from the model. This method might produce skilled artists and be a necessary part of training, but it did not produce the creativity that was all important for an illustrator. So, with his vast experience and his resolve to help young people get started on the right road, Pyle set out to develop a course that could produce men "who would paint living pictures rather than dead, inert matter in which there was not one single spark of real life."[1]

Steadfast in his belief that illustration was the basic art and the one that must be conquered before an artist could reach out and specialize, Pyle said: "Today I often find that the word 'illustrator' is regarded with contempt by a few who claim a higher position as being 'painters'. Such an attitude I cannot respect."[2]

The course at Drexel began on a simple note, a once-a-week gathering on Saturday afternoons at two o'clock. Only advanced students were accepted, and only after an evaluation of their ability. Approximately thirty students attended the initial course. Among them were three who were, within the not too distant future, to become outstanding in the field of illustration. Surprisingly for that day, two of these were women, Jessie Wilcox Smith and Elizabeth Shippen Green. The lone male in the trio was the fabulous Maxfield Parrish.

For its first two years, the Howard Pyle course was largely a trial run, but its success was so astounding that the circular of the School of Illustration for the 1896/7 semester announced:

After two years of experiment in conducting a class in Illustration at the Drexel Institute, under the direction of Mr. Howard Pyle, the results have been such as to warrant the Institute in extending considerably the scope of this branch of its work in the Art Department.[3]

Pyle's original intent had been to teach a small group for a few hours once a week—such a schedule would permit him to carry out his commitments to his publishers. But the course grew like the legendary beanstalk. The enlarged curriculum for the year 1896/7 dropped the original Saturday class and replaced it with Monday and Friday classes. Why was the course so successful? Originally, it may have been merely the magic of the Howard Pyle name that drew students, but as the aspiring illustrators promptly became aware of the high standards of performance demanded by their teacher, they recognized how uniquely valuable the course might prove to their future work.

Though the course was radical for its time, the principles it adhered to were simple. As already mentioned, the pupil gained admittance by passing an examination of his drawing ability; he was supposed to know the techniques of draftsmanship already. Beyond that, it was Pyle's main objective to teach his students how to project themselves, to put mind and body completely into the story to be told on canvas. Only in this way, Pyle was convinced, could the student create and not imitate. A second and no less important part of the course was mastering the technique of composition. His own experience had taught him that this was all-important for success.

Perhaps the most valuable contribution Howard Pyle made to his young charges was his own nature and character. His personality, his dedication to his art, and his deep spiritual sincerity influenced and inspired all those who studied under him. He was far more than a great teacher. He was counselor, guide, and—most important—a sincere friend.

Under Pyle's influence, the School of Illustration at Drexel soon expanded to the point where he felt he could no longer carry on the high ideals and standards that were his original intent. The classes grew too large, and he felt that only a minority of the students really had the qualities to carry on in the illustrating profession. He could not give these few the attention they merited without being accused of showing favoritism, and this he could not abide. In February of 1900 he wrote his resignation:

My time is very valuable, and now that I feel myself quite matured in my art knowledge, I think it both unwise and wrong to expend my time in general teaching. The great majority of a class as large as that which I teach at the Drexel Institute is hopelessly lacking in all possibility of artistic attainment. There are only one or two who can really receive the instruction which I give. To impart this instruction to these two or three who can receive it appears to be unfair to the others who do not receive such particular instruction. This apparent favoritism upon my part must inevitably tend to disrupt the Art School or to make the large majority discontented with the instruction which they receive in contrast with that which the few receive; nor is it possible to assure such discontented pupils that that which I give them is far more abundant and far more practical than that which they would receive from any other Art Institute—the fact remains in their minds that they are not given that which I give to the other pupils and that apparently there is favoritism in the class.[4]

When Howard Pyle resigned from Drexel, he had already formulated plans to open his own school in Wilmington, Delaware. The new school was to be built around those few exceptional young people who had studied under him at Drexel. By his personal invitation they followed him to Wilmington—Stanley Arthurs, Philip Hoyt, James McBurney, Ethel Franklin Betts, Sarah Stillwell, Ellen Thompson, and Frank E. Schoonover.

The program he intended to follow at Wilmington was basically the same as the one he had so successfully formulated at Drexel. He was, however, determined that the enrollment would remain limited to a carefully selected few. Those young artists who were capable of absorbing his theories of mental projection and of composition would have the greatest chance of working under his guidance. There were no entrance examinations as such. The student was simply advised to submit "examples" of his work: "When you apply for admission to the school, don't send me 'samples' of your work, send 'examples'. There are no 'samples' of art."[5]

These examples were carefully reviewed by Howard Pyle personally. If they showed "imagination and enthusiasm, artistic ability and drawing technique," the student could consider himself fortunate. This was the entrance examination, and as simple as it appeared on the surface it was an exacting test to meet. Of the hundreds of young people who applied to him for admittance, few were accepted.

It is our gain that one who was, was Newell Convers Wyeth.

# *Wyeth's Student Years*

NEWELL CONVERS WYETH was born in Needham, Massachusetts, on October 22, 1882.

Needham shared the colonial flavor of nearby towns whose names are better known because of historical events that brought them into more prominent focus—Plymouth, Salem, Lexington, Concord, and, of course, Boston. In the time of Wyeth's childhood, Needham was still a quiet suburban community, agricultural in flavor. The Wyeth farm, nestled on the banks of the Charles, had been operated by succeeding generations of the family ever since the homestead had been built in 1730.

Of his early life on the farm, Wyeth later recalled:

One of the greatest assets in my life has been the early training I received at home. My brothers and myself were expected to do every conceivable form of work about the home and in it. I find the earliest years of my life are the source of my best inspiration.[1]

The "chores" young Newell performed as a boy were to prove invaluable in his work in later

Sketchbook Self-portrait (circa 1896)
Drawing on paper, h:7, w:4½
Unsigned
Courtesy of Mr. & Mrs. Anton Kamp

SELF-PORTRAIT (1900)
Oil on canvas, h:24½, w:19½
Unsigned
Courtesy of Andrew Wyeth

years: he knew from personal experience the arrangement of a saddle on a horse, how to hold a scythe or wheat cradle, the proper method of log splitting and plowing.

Like most children, young Wyeth displayed an early interest in drawing pictures, but unlike most youngsters, who gradually are diverted to other pursuits, he continued to draw.

It's a strange thing, but I seemed to lack all that imaginative stuff that most kids have. I was quiet and my mother said I was observant, but I saw things as they were, and not as the fairy tales paint them.[2]

By the time Newell had reached his mid-teens, he knew that he wanted to be an artist. He must certainly have discussed this with those closest to him, but it was his mother who was the most sympathetic of anyone. When he was sixteen he was about to be sent off to New Hampshire to work as a farmhand, but she intervened and insisted that he be given an opportunity to develop his talent, and she prevailed. He was sent to the Massachusetts Normal Art School. There, Richard Andrew recognized the boy's natural inclination toward illustration and encouraged him in that direction. Wyeth said later:

I rose to his advice like a trout to a straw and soon attached myself to C. W. Reed, who was a book illustrator with a studio on West Street.[3]

Next the young man attended the Eric Pape School of Art, and in the spring of 1902 he began to study with Charles H. Davis in Mystic, Connecticut. However, though he had both talent and motivation, in his inexperience he did not realize that he was not receiving the proper training in the art of illustration. Twenty years later he was to mention this in an article he wrote:

To destroy individuality seems to be the main function of the illustrating classroom today. To turn the embryo mind face to face with technical methods, style, and the restrictions of publishing processes which all figure so prominently in composition, before he is able to feel the divine urge which comes only from a sound initiation into nature's truths is, to my mind, the

HOWARD PYLE'S STUDIO (March 1903)
Oil on canvas, h:12, w:8
Unsigned
Courtesy of Mr. & Mrs. Richard Layton

principal reason why such a tragic percentage of art students fail.

I know from experience what it means to answer that premature call for pictures. The second week I spent in an art school I was requested to do this as part of the routine, and how I suffered for that entire year. I noted that cleverness was rewarded, stunty and affected methods got the applause, so naturally I concluded that my salvation lay in my ability to develop a new "stunt".

Then he reflected back through the years to the time he was given the opportunity to study under Howard Pyle, and continued:

Only rarely does a fortunate student happen upon a helpful mind, one sufficiently strong and sympathetic to help him back into the real light.[4]

While Wyeth was a student at the Eric Pape School of Art, two of his close friends and classmates, Clifford Ashley and Henry Peck, were accepted as trial students in the Howard Pyle School of Art in Wilmington. They urged him to send some of his work to Pyle for evaluation. Because of the limitations Pyle placed on

[ 23 ]

the size of his class, young Wyeth felt he had little hope of acceptance, but he sent his drawings anyhow. To his delight, he was summoned to Wilmington.

It was "one of those blue and golden days in October. The air was sharp and keen,"[5] and it was also his twentieth birthday, October 22, 1902, a day he would long remember.

My most vivid recollecton of Howard Pyle was gained during the first five minutes I knew him. He stood with his back to the blazing and crackling logs in his studio fireplace, his legs spaced apart, his arms akimbo. His towering figure seemed to lift to greater heights with the swiftly ascending smoke and sparks from the hearth behind him.

I was young, ambitious and impressionable. For years, it seemed, I had dreamed of this meeting. Success in winning this master's interest and sympathy to the cause of my own artistic advancement seemed so much to ask, so remote, such a vain hope. But here I was at last, seated before him in the very room in which were born so many of the pictures I had breathlessly admired from boyhood. Paintings and drawings that had long since become a living and indispensable part of my own life.

And as Howard Pyle stood there, talking gently but with unmistakable emphasis, his large and genial countenance hypno-

tized me. My rapid reflections were swept beyond the actual man. It was bewildering. I heard every modulation of his voice and I took note of his every word. Occasionally I would answer a question. I remember all this clearly.

I had come to him, as many had before me, for his help and guidance, and his first words to me will forever ring in my ears as an unceasing appeal to my conscience: "My boy, you have come here for help. Then you must live your best and work hard!" His broad, kindly face looked solemn as he spoke these words, and from that moment I knew that he meant infinitely more to me than a mere teacher of illustration.[6]

The interview ended, and Wyeth was accepted as a pupil on probation.

I speculated for a week and then decided to stay on with him and was assigned a place to live and work. I had expected to hear Howard Pyle enthuse over my drawings, and to find him pass over them casually just about knocked the props from under me. The one note of encouragement was his interest in my background of New England living and the amount of enthusiasm I showed in wanting to come to him.[7]

The Howard Pyle School of Art was born of a thorough conviction that young people who had a truly earnest desire should be given the opportunity to benefit from the guidance and experience of one of the most highly respected and sought-after illustrators of the day. Pyle's motives were completely unselfish. There were no entrance fees or tuition at his school. The cost of materials and studio rental were nominal. But the requirements were stringent—imagination, artistic ability, a sense of color and drawing, youth, intelligence, and earnestness of purpose. Howard Pyle demanded hard work, but he also had a deep understanding of the needs of the young.

Howard Pyle *(center)* with a group of his students in 1903: George Harding, Gordon McCouch, Thornton Oakley, N. C. Wyeth, and Allen True. Courtesy of the Delaware Art Museum

There are many in this world who radiate the feeling of love and earnestness of purpose, but who have not the faculty or power to impart the rudiments of accomplishment. There is nothing in this world that will inspire the purpose of youth like the combined strength of spirituality and practical assistance. It gives the young student a definite clue, as it were, to the usefulness of being upright and earnest. Howard Pyle abounded in this power and lavished it upon all who were earnest.[8]

Mr. Pyle's inordinate ability as a teacher lay primarily in his sense of penetration; to read beneath the crude lines on paper the true purpose, to detect therein our real inclinations and impulses. Wretched, unstable drawing would quickly assume coherent shape and character; raw and uncouth conceptions would become softened and refined, until in a marvelously short time the student would find himself and emerge upon that elevation of thinking and feeling which would disclose before him a limitless horizon of possibilities.

The most striking feature of Mr. Pyle's teaching was his composition class. It met Monday evenings and each student was expected to bring a composition. This was a rough charcoal drawing made without

MAN WITH A PISTOL (1903)
Oil on canvas, h:29, w:22½
Signed lower right: N. C. Wyeth
Courtesy of Mrs. A. J. Sordoni, Jr.

models and intended to indicate a picture we wished to paint.[9]

The power of Howard Pyle stemmed from his wonderful interest in life: whether you painted it, or wrote about it, or lived it, the result must be vital, red-blooded, worthwhile. This love of life came through clearly in his work and in his teaching. According to former students, he used to tell them:

"It is easy enough to learn to draw; it is very difficult to learn to think." What he meant to express was, for us younger art students, the enormous difficulty of putting into a picture the essential qualities of deep feeling, sympathy and sincerity [that] far outweighed the lesser difficulty of accurately

Howard Pyle and students gathered in front of the old gristmill, Chadds Ford. Summer instruction was held here from 1898 to 1903.
Courtesy of the Delaware Art Museum

INTO TOWN FROM THE SOUTH
"Working for Fame," by John M. Oskison
*Leslie's Popular Monthly,* August 1903

glow, violet, then a dim, dusty gray? Who of us did not thrill in those moments when suddenly we heard the dull jar of the master's door, the slight after-rattle of the brass knocker as it closed, and the faint sound of his foot-steps on the brick walk? And then, as we had hoped, our own door was opened and he entered in the dim light and sat among us.

I can see him now, the soft overhead light faintly modeling his large, generous features, his massive forehead and deep-set eyes and the prominent cheek-bones. Breaking the tense silence he would talk in a soft, hushed voice of art, its relation to life, his aspirations, his aspirations for us. Only too soon he would say goodnight and leave us in the darkness, and, as we felt for our hats and coats, each one knew that every jaw was set to do better in life and work in some measure to express our deep gratitude to the one who had inspired us.[11]

learning to draw. Picture-making to Mr. Pyle was not making pictures of life but really putting down the life itself. He used to urge us to write as well as paint. "If you can picture life," he would say, "you can describe it."[10]

For the next four months young Wyeth put all his energies into his work. His reward came when his teacher informed him that his probation days were over and that he was now a full-fledged member of the Howard Pyle School. The young student was elated, but in sober reflection he later recalled little incidents that were especially meaningful in his striving to succeed and be accepted as a student under Pyle:

Who of his associates can forget the sombre hours in the gloaming when, after a hard day's work before our easels, we sat in the class studio, watching with blissful content the fading square patch of the skylight, warm with the light of the after-

Once young N. C. Wyeth had become an accepted member of the Howard Pyle School of Art, he took more time to look around. Older students, he noted, were already starting to carve profitable careers for themselves as illustrators, and so he decided to make an effort in that direction himself. He did a rough in oil in the grand manner—a wild bronco, pitching and twisting to unseat his rider—and from it made a finished canvas. This he submitted to the Curtis

BRONCO BUSTER
Oil on canvas, h:26, w:18
Signed lower right: Sketch 1902
Courtesy of the Delaware Art Museum

AS BROADWELL RACED WEST
"Working for Fame," by John M. Oskison
*Leslie's Popular Monthly,* August 1903

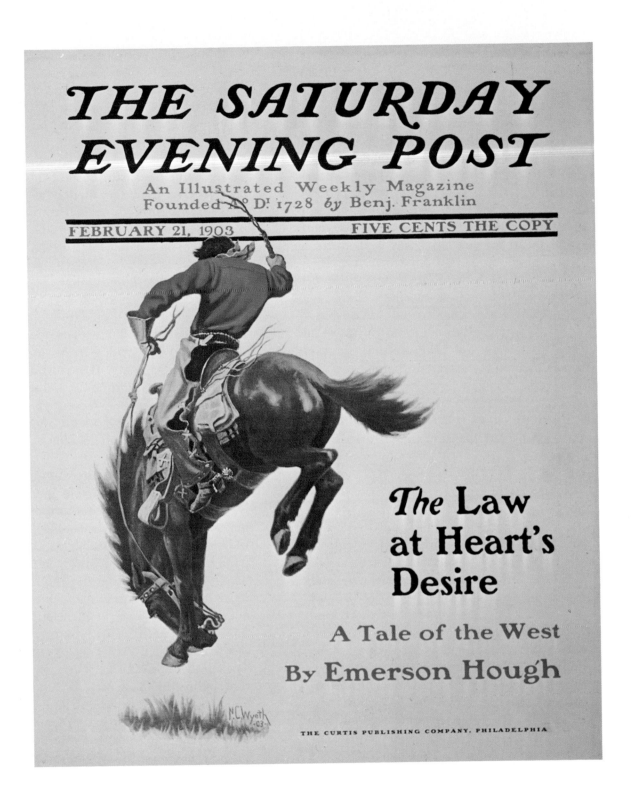

Publishing Company. On January 8, 1903, he could write: "The *Post* went wild over my cover and gave me $60 for it."

Several weeks later, he was disappointed to receive a check for $50 instead of the amount agreed upon, but his disappointment was short-lived when his painting finally appeared as the cover for *The Saturday Evening Post* of February 21, 1903. In the exuberance of youth, he felt he had arrived. Indeed, to have had a cover accepted and published by *The Saturday Evening Post* was no small accomplishment by any standard.

Wyeth did not rest on his laurels. He kept busily at work on other illustrations for other periodicals, and they were being accepted. The

March 1903 issue of *Success* published a story, "The Romance of the 'C.P.',", by Edwin Markham with an accompanying illustration by Wyeth. Untitled, it represented two surveyors at work during the construction of the Central Pacific Railroad, the theme of the story. The November and December issues of *Success* also contained Wyeth illustrations, as did the August 1903 issue of *Leslie's Popular Monthly*, for the story "Working for Fame" by John M. Oskison. This prompt recognition did not go to young Newell's head, however—he was well aware he still had much to learn from Howard Pyle.

Some of Wyeth's warmest memories pertained to this period of his life. There were parties. There were excursions into the surrounding area to rummage through old furniture and antique shops in search of interesting props and seasoned mahogany panels to paint upon. And there were frequent trips, especially in the warmer weather, to Mr. Pyle's home at Chadds Ford, Pennsylvania, where the students could roam the hills and woods of the historic Brandywine valley.

It was this remote village that brings back the fondest memories to the most of us. In a large roomy house that nestled in the trees beneath a great hill, within a stone's throw of General Lafayette's headquarters and surrounded by his wife and family of six children, I have the keenest and most enjoyable remembrances of him. Many, many jolly evenings did we spend before his crackling log fire, eating nuts, telling stories, or best of all listening to reminiscences of his own or accounts from his vast store of knowledge of history and of people. His intimacy with colonial his-

tory, and his sympathetic and authentic translations into pictures of those times are known and loved the world over.

How can I tell in words the life of the thirty or more of us who lived in these historic, rolling hills, working in the spacious and grain scented rooms of an old grist mill. To recall the unceasing rush of the water as it flowed over the huge, silent wheel beneath us thrills me through. And here the teacher kept his class intact for five glorious summers.[12]

Let it not be thought that the students in the Howard Pyle School of Art were different from other youths in their late teens and early twenties. They had their escapades too. One such incident was recalled by Wyeth during an interview in later years. It involved a fountain in Wilmington containing a sculptured cupid and a crane. In their "experienced minds," the students considered it bad art, badly proportioned and rather stupid looking.

So they improved its strangeness by adding a gay ballet skirt in many colors. Now there were certain authorities who did not approve of Cupids in ballet skirts and they took it upon themselves to analyze the paint thereon. Plainly it was from an artist's pallet, so the next thing the Cupid knew, a more or less contrite circle of art students, overseen by several laymen of the community, was industriously hiding the ballet skirt under a generous coat of white paint. The application of this paint was done so thoroughly that in a few days both Cupid and Crane were a mass of leprous-looking blisters. The very words are painful to think of, how much more so than the fountain itself. So of course there was nothing to be done but for the students to snatch it from its moorings and suspend it from a bridge over the river. The police, fearing that Cupid and his Crane might fall someday on a small foot-bridge that was nearby, cut the rope. Thus it came about that the fountain was assigned to complete and irretrievable oblivion.[13]

[ 28 ]

TWO SURVEYORS
"The Romance of the 'C.P.'" by Edwin Markham
*Success*, March 1903

N. C. Wyeth in the costume of Little John at the Howard Pyle Studio, March 4, 1904. The occasion was a banquet the students gave their teacher. From the Blanche Swayne Collection, Brandywine River Museum

FIGHTING THE FIRE FROM THE TELEPHONE POLES
Charcoal on paper
Signed lower right: Wyeth/Balto.
Feb–1904–
"The Great Baltimore Fire"
*Collier's Weekly,* February 13, 1904

AN EXHIBITION OF SELF EFFACEMENT . . .
"Take at the Flood," by Vincent Harper
*The Saturday Evening Post,* June 3, 1905

Howard Pyle believed in practical experience as part of the maturing process. An occasion to put this belief into practice came about quite suddenly. The disastrous Baltimore fire, which occurred in the early part of February 1904, was headline news. The Sunday morning of the fire a half dozen of the students were grouped around Mr. Pyle on the steps of his studio discussing the conflagration when he suddenly hit upon the idea of their going to Baltimore. As Wyeth later wrote, "If it became his impulse to carry out an idea, a scheme in our

THE MINUTE MEN
"Here once the embattled farmers stood and fired
the shot heard round the world."–Emerson
*The Delineator,* October 1905

... TRADING FROM THE BATTLEMENTED WALLS ...
"An Antiente Greate Companie," by Arthur E. McFarland
*The Saturday Evening Post,* November 1905

behalf, a trip, a banquet, nothing could stand in his way to accomplish it."[14]

Howard Pyle went to the phone, called the Collier office in New York, and arranged that his students cover the fire as sketch artists for the magazine. He put seventy-five dollars into their hands and they were shortly on their way.

Wyeth later commented: "Our sketches did not prove of any great value, although several were published, but our friend had thrust us in the way of some unique and valuable experience."[15]

An examination of numerous copies of *Collier's Weekly* issued during that period failed at first to bring to light any sketches of the Baltimore fire by the students. However, a drawing by N. C. Wyeth was printed in the magazine on February 13, 1904. Its rarity is due to the fact that it appeared in a separate supplement, and apparently fewer of these supplements were saved than of the regular issues.

The year 1904 was a relatively successful one for the young illustrator. His work also appeared in *Leslie's Popular Monthly, Metropolitan, The Saturday Evening Post, Scribner's,* and *Success.* One painting he began early that year merits special mention, though it did not appear in a magazine until the following year. Of it, he wrote: "I'm now deep in a successful picture of 'How the embattled farmers stood and fired the shot heard round the world.' I never enjoyed making a picture more in my life."

N. C. Wyeth, Stanley Arthurs, and Frank E. Schoonover were photographed in Atlantic City, New Jersey, by Allen True in 1906.
Courtesy of Frank E. Schoonover

THE BALL . . . ROLLED STRAIGHT TOWARD THE GOAL
Oil on canvas, h:34, w:24
Signed lower right: N. C. Wyeth '04
"Skiffington's Pony," by George Hibbard
*The Metropolitan,* October 1904
Courtesy of Kennedy Galleries, Inc., New York

This picture appeared in *The Delineator* in October 1905, but the appeal of the subject apparently remained with Wyeth, for he painted a strongly similar scene for one of the U.S. Treasury Department (bank holiday) posters he illustrated nearly two decades later.

The first book to contain Wyeth illustrations—*Boys of St. Timothy's* by Arthur Stanwood Pier—also made its appearance in 1904, but that year was memorable for other reasons too. In August he was graduated from the Howard Pyle School of Art and on his own, and in September he made his first trip west.

*The Saturday Evening Post* had commissioned Wyeth to illustrate a western story, and Howard Pyle also managed to convince *Scribner's Magazine* that the down-to-earth experience of a western trip for Wyeth might eventually prove advantageous to them, since he would be better able to provide authentic west-

ern illustrations for the magazine on future assignments. The result was that the *Post* and *Scribner's* jointly sponsored Wyeth's trip, an investment that ultimately more than paid for itself. His later illustrations for stories dealing with the West were without parallel for years, with the possible exception of the work Frederic Remington did exclusively for *Collier's Weekly.* It must be remembered, however, that the Remington paintings appearing in this magazine were, for the most part, documentary representations of an era long past.

The next chapter dwells on the work Wyeth did in the field of western illustration. His return East after the months spent in the Southwest did not affect his continuing in Wilmington under the guidance of Howard Pyle. For the next several years, in fact, he remained a member of that close-knit group of former students who were becoming well-known professionals.

Four Navajo studies young Wyeth made in November 1904.
Courtesy of Mrs. Andrew Wyeth

ROPING HORSES IN THE CORRAL
Oil on canvas, h:22, w:32
Signed lower left: N. C. Wyeth/Hash-knife Ranch/Colo
    1904
Courtesy of Dr. & Mrs. William A. Morton, Jr.

# 3

# N.C.'s West

Anyone familiar with the entire span of N. C. Wyeth's work cannot fail to be aware that even in his earliest drawings he showed a decided liking for picturing the Old West as he visualized it in his imagination. Like so many of us, he was completely fascinated by that era of American history.

It is reasonable to suspect that Wyeth's early inspiration for depicting the Old West may have been that great artist of the western scene Frederic Remington. Certainly, during his growing-up years, young Newell must have been exposed to many of Remington's pictures, for that indefatigable artist produced an endless stream of illustrations for all the leading periodicals of the day—*Harper's Weekly, Harper's Monthly, Century, Scribner's, Outing, Cosmopolitan, Youth's Companion,* and others. Later, while Wyeth was a student at the Howard Pyle School of Art, Remington's greatest works were

AN ALMIGHTY EXCITING RACE
"Arizona Nights," by Stewart Edward White
*McClure's Magazine,* March 1906

HAHN PULLED HIS GUN AND SHOT HIM THROUGH
THE MIDDLE
"Arizona Nights," by Stewart Edward White
*McClure's Magazine,* April 1906

appearing as full-color reproductions in *Collier's Weekly.* During those years too, it is known that whenever Wyeth had one of his infrequent opportunities to travel to New York, he never missed the chance to visit art galleries or the current exhibits, which at times were devoted exclusively to Remington's paintings.[1]

Although most of Wyeth's own first published works were strictly western in character, he had never been to the West to absorb its flavor and atmosphere and to gain the firsthand knowledge necessary to paint it with complete assurance and authenticity. Quite naturally, therefore, he welcomed the opportunity to make the western trip mentioned at the end of the preceding chapter, and he set out promptly in the latter part of September, the month following his graduation. For practical purposes, there was nothing else he could have done that would have proved more valuable, particularly since he

then seemed determined to do illustrations for western stories. By going there himself, he could observe with the keen eye of a good artist the people, the color, and the landscape.

During his visit in the West, he followed the trails into the mountains and the cattle country. He took part in all its work and pleasures, and managed to get a real taste of all the activities available, from carrying the mail and driving a stage to riding the range. He spent time at remote trading posts and with various Indian tribes, absorbing their customs and way of life and making careful observations of all he saw. And when he returned home, not only were his portfolios crammed with sketches; he also brought back saddles, bridles, guns, rugs, costumes, and regalia of all sorts for use in painting future pictures.

In the January 1906 issue of *Scribner's Magazine* it was noted that Mr. Wyeth had just

I SAW HIS HORSE JUMP BACK DODGIN' A
RATTLESNAKE OR SOMETHIN'
Oil on canvas, h:36, w:23¾
Signed lower left: N. C. Wyeth '05
"Arizona Nights," by Stewart Edward White
*McClure's Magazine,* April 1906
Courtesy of Southern Arizona Bank & Trust Company, Tucson

LISTEN TO WHAT I'M TELLIN' YE!
"Arizona Nights," by Stewart Edward White
*McClure's Magazine,* May 1906

N. C. Wyeth on horseback in Colorado, October 1904.
Courtesy of Frank E. Schoonover

returned from the West. The story of his experiences "in the cattle country engaged in the work of a cowboy in order to become thoroughly familiar with his subject" would be published in the not too distant future, the magazine promised. In strict accuracy, however, it must be pointed out that Wyeth had not "just returned from the West." He had returned at the end of December 1904.

Wyeth's article "A Day with the Round-Up" appeared in the March 1906 issue. Its color illustrations established him as a first-rate portrayer of the western scene, and his narrative proved him to be equally adept at writing. On the pages immediately following are reproduced both "A Day with the Round-Up" and the fine paintings that accompanied it in that memorable issue of *Scribner's Magazine.*

THE LAST STAND
Oil on canvas, h:50⅛, w:34
Signed lower left: N. C. Wyeth '06
"The Story of Montana," by C. P. Connolly
*McClure's Magazine*, September 1906
Courtesy of Southern Arizona Bank & Trust Company,
   Tucson

HANDS UP (*Holdup in the Canyon*)
Oil on canvas, h:43, w:30
Signed lower left: N. C. Wyeth '06
"The Story of Montana," by C. P. Connolly
*McClure's Magazine*, August 1906
Courtesy of Walter Reed Bimson, Valley National Bank,
   Phoenix, Arizona

[ 36 ]

THE PROSPECTOR
Oil on canvas, h:47, w:29¾
Signed lower left: N. C. Wyeth '06
"The Story of Montana," by C. P. Connolly
*McClure's Magazine*, September 1906
Courtesy of Southern Arizona Bank & Trust Company, Tucson

I HEREBY PRONOUNCE YUH MAN AND WIFE!
Oil on canvas, h:38, w:25
Signed lower left: N. C. Wyeth '07
"The Misadventures of Cassidy," by Edward S. Moffat
*McClure's Magazine*, May 1908
Courtesy of Mr. & Mrs. Joseph E. Levine

THE ADMIRABLE OUTLAW (My English friend thought
    it was a hold-up)
Oil on canvas, h:38, w:23½
Signed lower right: N. C. Wyeth, '06
"The Admirable Outlaw," by M'Cready Sykes
*Scribner's Magazine*, November 1906
Courtesy of the National Cowboy Hall of Fame and Western
    Heritage Center, Oklahoma City

[ 37 ]

RACING FOR DINNER

THE LEE OF THE GRUB-WAGON

ABOVE THE SEA OF ROUND, SHINY BACKS
THE THIN LOOPS SWIRLED

# *A Day with the Round-Up* *

Gʀᴏᴘɪɴɢ and feeling my way out from beneath three or four thick blankets and turning back to the stiff dewy tarpaulin, I peered into the gloom of early morning. The sweeping breeze of the plains brushed cool and fresh against my face. Shapeless forms of still sleeping men loomed black against the low horizon. Near by I saw the silhouetted form of the cook's thick legs and a big kettle swing before the light of the breakfast fire. I stared in wonderment about me—then my confused mind cleared and I remembered that it was the cow-camp of the night before.

I hurriedly pulled on my boots and

rolled the great pile of still warm blankets into a huge bundle and tied them so with two shiny black straps. Dark figures were moving about the camp—some crawling from beneath heaps of tangled beds, others trundling their big ungainly rolls, lifted high on their backs, to the bed-wagon. And so I carried mine, joining the silent processions that moved, a vague, broken line in the growing light of the early morning. . . .

Then I joined the dark mass of men around a tin pail of water. The cow-punchers do not wash very much on the round-up. A slap of water to freshen the face, a vigorous wipe with a rough, wearisome towel, and the men were ready for their breakfast.

I joined them—a crowd seated in the lee of the grub-wagon. Everything was very quiet, save now and then the click of the

* The illustrations used here appeared with the original article published in *Scribner's Magazine,* March 1906.

spoons on the tin cups. They ate in silence, all unconscious of the rich yellow glow that was flooding the camp.

Then the quiet of the morning was broken by a soft rumbling that suddenly grew into a roar, and from a great floating cloud of golden dust the horse herd swung into the rope corral.

The men tossed the tin cups and plates in a heap near the big dish-pan. There was a scuffle for ropes and the work started with a rush. In the corral the horses surged from one side to the other, crowding and crushing within the small rope circle. Above the sea of round, shiny backs, the thin loops swirled and shot into volumes of dust; the men wound in and out of the restless mass, their keen eyes always following the chosen mounts. Then one by one they emerged from the dust, trailing very dejected horses. The whistling of ropes ceased, and with a swoop the horse herd burst from the corral to feed and rest under the watchful eye of the "wrangler."

By now we had all "saddled up" and mounted save "The Swede." . . .

We watched him as he led his mount into "open country," for the horse was known to be "bad." His name was "Billy Hell," and he looked every bit of that. He was white, of poor breed, and probably from the North.

"The Swede" walked to the nigh side of his horse and hung the stirrup for a quick mount. . . . The horse stood perfectly still, his hind legs drawn well under him; his head hung lower and lower, the ears were flattened back on his neck, and his tail was drawn down between his legs. "The Swede" tightened his belt, pulled his hat well down on his head, seized the cheek-strap of the bridle with one hand, and then carefully fitted his right over the shiny metal horn. For an instant he hesitated, and then, with a glance at the horse's head, he thrust his boot into the iron stirrup and swung himself with a mighty effort into the saddle.

The horse quivered and his eyes became glaring white spots. His huge muscles gathered and knotted themselves in angry response to the insult. Then with his great brutish strength he shot from the ground, bawling and squealing in a frantic struggle to free himself of the human burden. It was

like unto death. Eight times he pounded the hard ground, twisting and weaving and bucking in circles. The man was a part of the ponderous creaking saddle; his body responded to every movement of the horse, and as he swayed back and forth he cursed the horse again and again in his native tongue.

Then it was over. The cow-punchers nodded in approval and one of them dropped from his saddle and picked up "The Swede's" hat.

"Rounding-up" means to hunt and to bring together thousands of cattle scattered over a large part of the country known as the free range. For convenience in hunting them, the free range is divided into a number of imaginary sections. Into these sections the "boss" of an outfit sends the score or more of punchers, divided into squads of twos and threes, each squad covering a given section. This is called "riding the circle." . . .

[One] morning I started out with the others on the trail of some four or five hundred cattle.

We rode many miles, finding every little while a few of the cattle, some three or four, perhaps, standing quietly together in a gully. And as we pushed our way toward the distant camp of the outfit that had moved to the farther end of the section since we left, our herd gradually increased. With the added numbers the driving became difficult and we had to crowd our horses into the rear of the sullen and obstinate herd. We crossed, recrossed, and crossed again, yelling and cursing and cutting them with our quirts. The herd slowly surged ahead, above them floating a huge dense cloud of silvery dust that seemed to burn under the scorching sun of the plains.

It was well-nigh to noon before we saw a sharp dark line on the horizon that appeared and disappeared as we rose and fell along the undulating creek bottom. We knew the dark line to be the cattle already rounded up, and that we were late. But we had ridden the big circle that morning.

Our cattle soon saw the larger herd, and their heads went up, their tails stiffened, and they hurried to join the long dark line that began slowly to separate itself, as we drew nearer, into thousands of

BUCKING

ROUNDING-UP

cattle. And as we approached the main herd our cattle became more quiet. From the distant waiting multitude, as if in greeting, came a low, rumbling moan. The sound was faint; it became audible as the hot wind of the plains blew against my face, then it died away again—even as the wind spent itself on the long stretch of level plain.

Soon our cattle were on the run, and from a distance we stopped and watched the two herds merge one into the other. We were late, and the cow-punchers greeted us with jibes of all sorts, but we did not mind them, for the day's drive was over. To the right of the herd, some six hundred yards, stood the grub-wagon. Near by it I saw the smoke slowly rising from the cook's fire, and my appetite was made ravenous. Someone called, "Who says dinner?" and with that came the stinging crack of many quirts, the waving of hats, the whirling of ropes, and with the cow-boys' yells . . . there followed a wild, spectacular race for dinner. My horse was tired and streaked with sweat and white dust, his ears drooped, his tail hung limp, and he breathed hard, but I found myself in the first "bunch" at the finish. I jumped to the ground and hurriedly loosened the saddle and the soaking wet blanket from the horse's back and threw them on the ground to dry. Then I made for the soap-box of tin dishes and heaped my tin plate with meat and potatoes, and afterwards, by way of dessert, I had a small can of tomatoes. We sat in the shade of the grub-wagon, and along with the eating the men told of a large herd of antelope they had seen and of an unbranded cow they had brought in.

The "wrangler" ended the dinner. Into the camp he drove the horse herd, and from it fresh mounts were roped for the afternoon's work of "cutting out."

Cutting out is a hard, wearisome task. There were some six thousand cattle in the herd that had been rounded up that morning, and it was the work of the men to weave through that mass and to drive out certain brands known as the "Hash Knife," the "Pot Hook," the "Lazy L," and the like.

The herd that had been quiet was again in a turmoil, bellowing and milling, but it was kept within limited bounds and well "bunched" by the score or more of punchers outside.

My roan was well trained. He seemed to know by my guiding which cow I was after, and with incredible twisting and turning, well-directed kicks and bites, we would separate our cow from the writhing mass. I could faintly see my fellow-workers, flat silhouettes in the thickening dust, dodging and turning through the angry mass of heads and horns. My throat grew parched and dry, and the skin on my face became tight and stiffened by the settling dust. . . .

And so the afternoon passed quickly. I rode for the last time into the sullen herd, carefully watching for any remaining cows with the brand of the "Hash Knife." But I did not find any; my work was finished and I rested in the saddle, watching the remaining men complete their "cutting out," helping them now and then with a stray cow.

The sun was low and very red, the shadows were long and thin. The afternoon's work was completed, and I was glad. From across the plain I saw the red dust of a small herd that had already left camp on their long night journey to the home pasture, and I heard the faint yelps of the cowboys who were driving them. I dismounted

and with the knotted reins thrown over my arm, slowly walked back to the grub-wagon.

Some of the beds had already been unrolled, and I spread mine in a good level place. The ground was still hot and dry, but the air was rapidly becoming cooler, and the dew would soon fall.

In twos and threes the men came into camp, tired and dusty. We grouped about the wagons, sitting on the tongues, on unrolled beds, anywhere, perfectly contented, watching the cook prepare the evening meal. The odor of coffee scented the air, and I was hungry and tired as I never was before.

After the supper, a circle of men gathered about the camp-fire. The pulsing glow of many cigarettes spotted the darkness; the conversation slowly died with the fire, and one by one the dark, sombre faces disappeared from the light.

I was the last to leave. I crawled into my blankets and lay for a moment looking into the heavens and at the myriads of stars. I pulled the blankets up to my chin and then I felt the warmth of the ground creep through them. As I lay there I heard the faint singing of a night herder floating across the plains, and—for an instant—I thought of the morrow.

CUTTING OUT

A NIGHT HERDER

BILLY THE KID and BOB OLLINGER
Headpiece pen-and-ink drawings
"The Imitation Bad Man," by Emerson Hough
*The Saturday Evening Post,* January 20, 1906

The illustrations accompanying Wyeth's first-person narrative "A Day with the Round-Up" must have been to some extent responsible for the subsequent constant demand for his talents in the field of western illustration. But even before that article was published in 1906, commissions for western pictures had poured in. In fact, from the time he returned from the West at the end of 1904, publishers had besieged him with requests.

*The Saturday Evening Post,* which had helped to finance the western trip, engaged Wyeth to illustrate three stories by Emerson Hough. The first, titled "The Wasteful West," appeared in the issue of October 14, 1905. "The Imitation Bad Man" and "The Tenderfoot" appeared in the issues of January 20 and February 10, 1906, respectively.

Stewart Edward White's great western classic *Arizona Nights,* illustrated by Wyeth, was originally published in three consecutive issues of *McClure's Magazine* in 1906. The first installment came out the same month as "A Day with the Round-Up"; the others, in the two months immediately following. Other notable Wyeth-illustrated short stories published in 1906 included "Bar 20 Range Yarns" by Clarence Edward Mulford (*Outing Magazine*) and "The Admirable Outlaw" by M'Cready Sykes (*Scribner's Magazine*).

Unlike *Arizona Nights,* which first appeared serially in a magazine and then was published as a book, four great western stories that Wyeth illustrated appeared only in book form. Two of these, *The Throwback* by Alfred Henry Lewis and *Whispering Smith* by Frank H. Spearman, were published in 1906; the other two, *Langford of the Three Bars* by Kate and Virgil D. Boyles and *Beth Norvell* by Randall Parrish, appeared in 1907. However, in spite of his prodigious output of western illustration from 1905 through 1907, he still found time to illustrate numerous other works that were not western in character.

Wyeth undertook the only other trip he ever made into the Far West in the early part of 1906. Of short duration, it was sponsored by *Outing Magazine,* for Wyeth to do a series of paintings for an article, "How They Opened the Snow Road," by W. M. Raine and W. H. Bader. Four color plates accompanied the article in the January 1907 issue of that magazine. (They are reproduced here in black and white in Chapter 8.)

Of the other great western illustrations Wyeth made over the next few years, some were done for stories and others stood by themselves as frontispiece color plates. Several of the best of these are reproduced in this chapter.

In the January 1909 issue of *Scribner's Magazine,* Wyeth's second autobiographical narrative appeared—"A Sheep-Herder of the South-West." This was drawn from recollections of his first trip west in 1904. The narrative was supplemented by several of his finest western works, more easel art than illustration.

HUNGRY, BUT STERN, ON THE DEPOT PLATFORM
"The Imitation Bad Man," by Emerson Hough
*The Saturday Evening Post,* January 20, 1906

A PARTNERSHIP FOR THE SAKE OF GREATER
    SAFETY
Oil on canvas, h:16, w:36
Signed lower left, Wyeth '05
"The Wasteful West," by Emerson Hough
*The Saturday Evening Post,* October 14, 1905

THE PAY STAGE
Oil on canvas, h:38, w:26½
Signed lower right: N. C. Wyeth, March '09
*Scribner's Magazine,* August 1910
Courtesy of Southern Arizona Bank & Trust Company, Tucson

NAVAJO HERDER IN THE FOOTHILLS
Oil on canvas, h:37¼, w:28¼
Signed lower right: N. C. Wyeth '08
Collection of Douglas Allen, Jr.

# A Sheep-Herder of the South-West*

Two Gray Hills," a remote Navajo Indian trading-post in New Mexico, looks for all the world like a play-village of tiny squared mud-cakes, built on a vast, undulating play-ground of sand hills, with a long, low strip of blue-paper mountains slid in behind it. And not until you get within calling distance of the "Post" can you fully determine its identity. In reality it is mud, with a few small windows pierced in three of its sides resembling port-holes, and a dirt roof, growing a veritable garden of grass and weeds, out of which peeps the top of a gray stone chimney. To the right of the

building stand two low adobe barns, and to the left a long, flat sheep-shed, fraying off into a spindly corral.

As I came upon "Two Gray Hills" one warm October afternoon, after two days of slow, thirsty travel across the desert from Farmington, Sel Ritchie, trader, received me with the hearty hospitality so characteristic of these remote merchants of the desert; and after I explained to him my great interest in the Indians and anxiety to see something of their life, he instantly invited me to make his "Post" my headquarters.

What a remarkable vantage-point it was! Surrounding us and extending endlessly to the east lay the great gray desert, the sky-line broken by freakish shapes of earth and rock and the tumbled ruins of

* The illustrations accompanying this narrative by N. C. Wyeth appeared with the original article in *Scribner's Magazine,* January 1909.

ancient Pueblo dwellings that bore strange tales of superstition and encounter; and hidden below the gray levels, in the canyons and arroyos, were mysterious caves, poisonous springs, and enchanted pools, the sight and scene of many Indian festivities and ceremonies.

And to the west of the "Post," not half a day's ride, stretched the Pine Ridge, an imposing range of jagged mountains, the home of many cold, sparkling brooks, grassy uplands, shady groves of cottonwoods, fragrant pine forests, and great spreading groups of nut-laden piñon trees.

Hidden amidst this abundance are sequestered many Navajo settlements of dome-shaped huts, built of mud and logs; thatch-roofed sheep-barns, large corrals of gnarled roots and brush; and like gems laid deep in slumbrous colors, one would often come upon blanket weavers seated before ponderous looms, upon which would be stretched blankets of brilliant scarlet and black, or blue and white; and mingled with the chatter of the weavers or the calls of the children one could always hear the distant musical tinkle of the sheep-bells, as the many herds wandered above and below on the steep slopes of the mountain-sides.

This remote tinkle of bells was from the first fascinating and alluring to me; so one morning, while roaming around the mountains, I decided to hunt out one of the roving bands and its keeper. For three hours I climbed over ledges, crawled through thickets, crossed innumerable mountain streams, toward that always far-away tinkle; but not until the noon-day sun threw its shortest shadows did I discover that my quest was an echo; that I had climbed the wrong side of the ravine.

It was too late that day to resume the search, but on the morrow, after a delightful night's sleep under the venerable roof of a mighty pine grove, I found my will-o'-the-wisp.

From my night's resting-place, in the cool morning shadows at the base of the long deep slope, I could distinctly hear the silvery ring of that elusive bell from far above where the morning sun shone and where the dews sparkled. How I wished I could be invisibly and silently placed amid that mountain pastoral, without disturbing the unconscious peacefulness of it all; could absorb that vision of poetry without intruding my commonplace self to disconcert the herder, to frighten the sheep, and arouse the watchful dog.

As I feared, my entrance upon the scene spoiled it all. But, thanks to my almost noiseless approach, I was able first to get at least a glimpse of the life with all its charm.

Before a small fire, its thin, blue skein of smoke floating upward on the light morning air, kneeled a Navajo boy; he was about twelve years old, his bobbed hair hung down to his shoulders in a dense mass, which was held back from his eyes with a deep crimson "bandy" of silk tied around his head. He wore a faded blue blouse, belted in very low on the hips with a frayed sash. Tight trousers, split from the knee down on the outside, a little the worse for wear, and a pair of smoke-tanned moccasins completed his costume. Beside him, in a heap, lay his blanket of many colors, and upon it his bow and quiver of arrows. On a long, slender spit he was roasting a piece of meat, which was eagerly watched by a big, shaggy dog seated close at his side. Behind this group and running at a slant up the mountain-side were the sheep, busily feeding. The bell, even at so close range, sounded soft and muffled, and I wondered that the sound could carry as far as I knew it did.

But this fragment of unconscious beauty lasted but a brief moment. My presence was discovered. The dog barked and bounded toward me, the boy jumped to his feet and gathered his blanket about him, the sheep ceased their quiet feeding and disappeared into the thickets. The dog's threatening behavior occupied my attention for a few moments; meanwhile the boy, my prize, had fled; and when the dog discovered that he was left alone with me, he turned and scampered likewise.

For a long time I sat there and listened to the diminishing sound of the bell, until finally, far up in the heights, I heard the slow, uneven chime telling me that peace and quietude reigned once more. I hadn't courage to molest them again, so retraced my tracks down the mountain, took my horse at one of the settlements at its base, and reached "Two Gray Hills" that evening. Of course I related my experience to Ritchie, and it apparently struck him as being wholly to be expected. He related similar experiences of his own, and practically discouraged me from ever trying to become in the least familiar with the Indians.

One morning, not long after, I was in the corral trying to rope an old, scraggly, moth-eaten looking burro. I had caged my droll target, and resolved to practise a new throw upon it until I at least understood the method. I had made about half a dozen very crude and unsuccessful attempts, and was preparing my rope for the next one when my captive made a run for the gate. The bar I knew was too high for the stiff-legged burro to jump—but lo and behold! he made a sort of running slide and rolled under it. I saw his trick quick enough to make a ragged, awkward cast, and as luck would have it, my loop made fast to a kicking hind leg just as he rolled under the bar. This sudden success came as a surprise, but the surprise that immediately followed had it "beaten a mile"—his triphammer kicks jerked the rope out of my hand, and away he galloped, stiff-legged and awkward like a calf, with my new hemp and horse-hair rope dangling and snapping after him. I watched him with disgust until he disappeared in a cloud of dust, my chief thought being a hope that no one had witnessed this "tenderfoot" predicament; but no sooner had it flashed through my mind than I heard behind me a shrill, boyish laugh, and, turning, whom should I see, looking through one of the larger openings, but my sheep-herder from the mountains. I felt humiliated. I tried to intercept his continued laughter with an explanation, but he wouldn't listen, and suddenly left me and disappeared in the big door of the "store".

Disgusted, I made a detour of the post buildings, thinking perhaps that I might locate the burro on the near-by sandhills; but he had fled from sight, so I, too, strolled

[ 47 ]

into the store, determined to face out my discomfiture. There were a number of Indians inside, and when I entered they greeted me with broad, knowing grins and started talking about me among themselves. I felt like a spanked child. The boy stood over behind the big chunk-stove, his black eyes sparkling with delight. I smiled at him, and he grinned back, disclosing two rows of handsome teeth that looked like pearls against the mahogany-copper colored skin of his face, and his hair looked blacker than ever. His shining eyes followed every movement I made, and I perceived that he was intently looking at my watch-fob, a miniature stirrup of silver.

The older Indians, as they finished the bargaining, departed one by one, and finally there remained only the trader, the boy and myself. Now was my chance! I asked Ritchie

THE PLAINS HERDER
Oil on canvas, h:37¼, w:28¼
Signed lower left: N. C. Wyeth 1908
Courtesy of Southern Arizona Bank & Trust Company, Tucson

at Ford Defiance for two years, and could talk freely if he wanted to.

Further efforts proved useless, but Begay continued to follow me around, always placing himself within sight of the silver stirrup dangling from my watch-pocket. At last I hit upon a plan. I would give him the stirrup. To see his face light up, to watch his big black eyes dance with pleasure, was worth fifty watch-fobs. With a grunt of satisfaction, he snatched the treasure from my hand, and concealing it in his blouse dashed out of the store.

It was only after a long search that I found him seated on the ground behind the wood-pile, gazing at the trinket with all his eyes, placing his finger in the tiny stirrup, holding it up by the strap with the other hand, and turning it in the sun to see it shine and glisten. His face this time met mine with a gracious smile; little by little I urged him to talk; and before the afternoon wore away we became fast friends.

That night Ritchie told me that the boy was about to trail a thousand sheep twenty-five miles across the desert to "Nip" Arment's, a sheep buyer and cattle dealer, just off the reservation; and had come, in anticipation of his trip, to make arrangements to corral and feed the sheep for one night, as he expected to make "Two Gray Hills" his first stopping place.

Such an undertaking for so young a boy seemed to me incredible, but I was told that he had accomplished the same thing for the two previous years, and once with two thousand sheep. And, furthermore, he always went on foot, which to me made the achievement even more remarkable. Ritchie could not understand my desire to accompany the lad on such a wearisome journey, but, according to my wishes he promised to "fix it up" so that I could go.

Three evenings later, a thin drift of dust appeared directly in the light of the setting sun, and by eight o'clock a thousand bleating sheep were driven into the cedar corral for the night. Many loosened bales of alfalfa were thrown in for them to eat, and the long, shallow troughs were filled with water. The boy was accompanied by his father to this point, who stopped only long

to explain to the boy who I was and in some way break the ice toward an acquaintance. At this request Ritchie laughed and the boy grinned. "He kin talk Americano as good as you and me kin; go ahead an' hit up a pow-wow with him," said Ritchie, and added, "His name is Begay."

At this glad news I turned to Begay and burst into a flow of explanations and questions. The boy stood mute, looking at me blankly, and after a long pause he answered in a soft half-whisper: "No savvy." I tried in every way to induce him to talk, but these were the only words he would utter. His continued silence and occasional solemn glances at Ritchie almost convinced me that the "trader" was playing a little joke on his guest; but I was reassured that the boy had attended the government school enough to see the sheep safely corralled, and with a few parting words to Begay disappeared into the night toward his distant cornfields in the bottom-lands, where his squaws had already started the harvesting.

We started two hours before sun-up. The bars of the corral were lifted out, the dog wormed his way among the still sleeping herd, and suddenly the dim, gray mass poured out of the gate, turned a sharp angle to the left and streamed off into the darkness. A few quick, mysterious words from the boy sent the dog hurtling after. Begay, his blanket girded about his loins with an old cartridge-belt, a small haversack of buckskin hung over one shoulder, and a curious stick from which dangled a number of empty tomato-cans, suspended by thongs, left us without a word in the direction of the vanished herd; and with a hurried "so long" to Ritchie I followed him.

The long, hard journey had begun. Dust arose from the herd in clouds; I could not see it, but could feel it sift against my face, and I could taste the peculiar, sweet flavor of alkali. Frequent calls from the boy to his dog, punctuated by the occasional clatter of the tin cans on the stick was all that broke the silence beyond the soft, quivering rustle made by thousands of feet as they plodded through the sand.

The level horizon of the desert lay before us, toward which we slowly trudged through endless stretches of loose sand, around the bases of towering buttes and down into and out of many dry arroyos. It was in these places that I saw Begay put the mysterious stick with its jingling cans into effective use. To drive the sheep over the banks and down into the dry river beds was an easy matter, but to force them up the sharp acclivity on the opposite side required considerable strategy. As the herd approached the embankment, it would invariably turn either to the right or left and run along the base of it, vainly searching for easier footing. At a word from Begay, the well-trained dog would dash to the front of the bunch, frantically jumping and barking, nipping the legs of the leaders, and eventually turning the entire herd in

NOTHING WOULD ESCAPE THEIR BLACK, JEWEL-LIKE, INSCRUTABLE EYES
Oil on canvas, h:46½, w:37½
Signed lower left: N. C. Wyeth
"Growing Up," by Gouverneur Morris
*Harper's Monthly Magazine,* November 1911
Courtesy of Edward Eberstadt & Sons, New York

the opposite direction. Then the boy from his position between the sheep and the open stretch of the arroyo, waving his blanket and hissing loudly, would hurl his stick and jingling cans in front of the sheep fast escaping through the unguarded side. The cans would jangle and crash on the stones and hard gravel, and the panic-stricken animals, frightened by the noise, would scramble up the bank, Begay would recover his "tanglang" as he called it, and we would laboriously crawl up after them.

The trip had been one of very few words; those that had passed between us could be numbered on the fingers of one hand. Twice, with solemn gesture, he pointed out distant landmarks, and explained, in short, quick accent, "Toh," meaning water; and another time he fondly pulled the silver stirrup from inside his blouse, and, holding it up, smiled and questioned, "To qui?" meaning "how much?" I did not comprehend exactly what he meant, although I could interpret the words. Finally I answered, fully an hour

[ 49 ]

later, "Peso," meaning one dollar. At this he smiled a broad, pleased smile, and from then on he would take out the ornament again and again, and holding it in the sunlight would watch it glisten, casting laughing sidelong glances at me.

Except for these few moments of slight diversion, Begay's attention was fixed steadfastly on his sheep, his eyes always watchful of the condition of the trail ahead. Toward the end of the afternoon he urged the sheep on at a faster pace, and frequently looked at the position of the sun.

His anxiety evidently grew greater as it neared the horizon, and once I questioned him about the distance to water, but he was silent and seemed not to be conscious of my presence.

The slow, steady walking since four o'clock that morning, with not even a halt for noon lunch, through heavy sands, up steep slopes, and over rough mounds of shale-rock and loose gravel, began to tell on me. My thighs at times became cramped and stiff, and for miles I would walk stooped in order to proceed at all. And now, as the herd increased its speed to almost double, I was gradually left behind. Begay appeared as fresh as in the early morning. He walked with perfect ease and grace, his long, slender legs measuring off the distance in rhythmic steps, his body bent slightly forward, one arm clasping his blanket and "tanglang," and the other swinging free like a pendulum.

I managed to stagger along for an hour more with the herd well in the lead; the sun had disappeared behind a deep purple horizon, and the afterglow flooded the desert with a radiant, liquid light. All the earth glowed as though lighted from within, the very sands at my feet looked a stained

orange, and the few clumps of dry, dusty sage-brush fairly burned in the weird light; while far ahead, just over the margin of a low hill, a great, red, golden cloud of dust told the tale of the fast-moving herd.

Twenty minutes of weary, anxious plodding brought me to the summit; the light was growing dim, but I could vaguely see, 'way down the gentle slope, a fringe of cedar clumps, and from beyond them I could hear the faint murmur of the sheep, like distant strains of many bagpipes. I knew they were nearing water; and I felt so relieved at the thought that it was comparatively near that I lay down in my tracks, and in perfect contentment watched the stars as they appeared one by one.

I don't know how long it was before I was suddenly conscious of a distant call; the sound drew nearer until I recognized the boyish voice of Begay. He had returned to find me, and as we slowly made our way in the dark, he told me in his own quaint way the reason of his anxiety and hurry: "Sheep no drink for long time—dark come quick—afraid for no find trail to water in deep hole—sheep run and fall on rock—get kill." And with a long impressive pause, "Me no want kill sheep—Savvy?"

I understood, but I understood far better when we cautiously picked our way down one of the most precipitous trails I ever saw. How he managed to get those thousand restless, thirsty sheep down into that canyon, fully two hundred feet deep, unscathed, as they proved to be, is far beyond my imagination. It was incredible!

We ourselves crawled down, and frequently I lighted matches to see where to place my foot next, sick, dizzy, to see the edge of the trail not a foot away disappearing into a chasm of blackness. Now and then a loose piece of shale would slide off into space, and it seemed minutes before the dry click sounded as it struck the bottom.

Once at the base, Begay led me to a large log "hogan," similar to the dome-shaped huts I had seen in the mountains. We crawled through the low door, and soon had a cheery fire of crackling cedar logs burning in the center of the floor, the smoke rising and disappearing out of the large vent in the roof. This shelter had been built for the use of any-one who found it

MEXICAN SHEPHERD
Oil on canvas, h:28¼, w:37¼
Signed lower left: N. C. Wyeth 1908
Courtesy of Southern Arizona Bank & Trust Company, Tucson

necessary to spend the night in the canyon. On one side were piled two or three dozen ragged and worn sheep skins for bedding, and alongside, piled in a heap on the ground, were a number of blackened and dented tin dishes. In the center sat a great pile of wood-ashes, telling the tale of many camp-fires, and over the low door hung a tattered piece of buckskin. We made a pot of strong, black coffee from the muddy water, from which a stench of sheep now rose, and with a large can of veal-loaf and some pilot bread we ate ravenously until barely enough was left for breakfast. With the last mouthful swallowed, the boy dragged four or five skins to the fire, and wrapping himself in his blanket threw himself upon them, and immediately fell into a sound sleep. The night promised to be a sharp, frosty one, so I dragged a huge cedar root on to the dying embers, and preparing in my turn a bed of skins was soon dead to the world.

It seemed hardly an hour's time before I was aroused by the bark of the dog and the bleating sheep. I crawled out of the hut wrapped in my blanket; it was still dusk, but the sky was rapidly brightening. A sharp, cutting wind swept through the canyon, and I could hear Begay down at the water-hole cracking the ice with a stick. The high rock walls that hemmed us in loomed gigantic and black in the gloom; they resembled the ruins of mighty castles, fringed at the top with the silhouettes of tufted cedar. The steady increasing gray light sifted down upon us, disclosing enormous rounded boulders, jagged pinnacles of rock, mysterious caves, gnarled and twisted cedars through which the winds moaned and sighed, drifting the loose sands in tiny eddies into caves and crevices or piling it in fantastic mounds on the open stretches. Directly behind the hut, and protected by a projecting ledge, nestled the corral enclosing the sheep, and beyond, at the foot of a long, gentle incline, lay the precious pool of water.

A light breakfast eaten and the sheep watered, we started the second and last lap of our journey. Unlike the descending trail of the previous night, the way out of the

canyon was comparatively easy, except that we had to be very cautious and evade the many soft and treacherous sand-drifts. I asked Begay what time he expected we would reach our destination; he replied by pointing to the sun and following its orbit till its position indicated three o'clock.

It was about that time when we descended into the bottom-lands of the Rio Las Animas, where lay "Nip" Arment's thriving trading-post.

The sheep moved slowly, and the dog, his services unneeded, lagged behind. We were seen long before we reached the post, and upon our arrival a dozen Indians aided Begay to count and corral the sheep. I stood apparently unnoticed, until, as all were walking toward the "store," Begay flourished the silver stirrup; a brief explanation followed and all eyes were turned on me.

A moment later "Nip" Arment appeared upon the scene, and with a hearty welcome led me to his house. The home was lavish in comforts; many Navajo rugs adorned the floors, numberless trophies of the hunt and rare relics from the desert hung on the walls; but I missed my new friend. That night I talked long and late with the trader, and once in bed I fell into a sound, sound sleep. I did not wake before noon; but then I dressed hurriedly and rushed out in search of Begay. A group of Indians were playing cards behind the "store" in the warm sun, and I asked them where to find him. One of them, a tall, sinister fellow, slowly and solemnly arose, and coming over to where I was standing, placed one hand on my shoulder and pointed with a long, dark finger at two disappearing specks on the western horizon. They were Begay and his dog.

PASTORAL OF THE SOUTH-WEST

CALLING THE SUN DANCE
Oil on canvas, h:35½, w:26½
Signed lower left: N. C. Wyeth '08
Courtesy of W. S. Farish III

INVOCATION TO THE BUFFALO HERDS
Oil on canvas, h:36, w:26
Signed lower right: N. C. Wyeth
Courtesy of the Armand Hammer Foundation

Shortly after returning from his journey to Colorado in 1906, Wyeth felt the urge to settle down in his own peaceful area of Chadds Ford, Pennsylvania. The West had been good for him and for his pursuit, but the lengthy absences from home and family made him long for a more settled way of life.

... with five years of almost incessant work, mostly western in character, I have experienced a remarkable change. My ardor for the West has slowly, but with increasing impetus, been dwindling, until my desires to go there to paint its people are already lukewarm. The West appealed to me as it would to a boy; a sort of external effervescence of spirit seemed to be all that substantiated my work.[2]

But the demand for his western illustrations was to plague him for years to come. Publishers continued to vie for his talents in this field, and he was sometimes deluged with requests to illustrate books and stories in periodicals and to make western-type pictures for commercial art commissions as well. Among the books for which he painted western scenes were *Reminiscences of a Ranchman* by Edgar Beecher Bronson (1910), *Letters of a Woman Homesteader* by Eleanor Pruitt Stewart (1914), *Nan of Music Mountain* by Frank H. Spearman (1916), *Vandemark's Folly* by Herbert Quick (1922), *The Oregon Trail* by Francis Parkman (1925), and *Ramona* by Helen Hunt Jackson (1939). The western classic *Cimarron* by Edna Ferber, which was published serially by *Woman's Home Companion* from November 1929

[ 53 ]

THE ORE WAGON
Oil on canvas, h:38, w:25
Signed lower right: N. C. Wyeth '07
"The Misadventures of Cassidy," by Edward S. Moffat
*McClure's Magazine,* May 1908
Courtesy of Southern Arizona Bank & Trust Company, Tucson

I'VE SOLD THEM WHEELERS
"The Misadventures of Cassidy," by Edward S. Moffat
*McClure's Magazine,* May 1908

A FIGHT ON THE PLAINS
Oil on canvas, h:32, w:40
Signed lower right: To Mr. and Mrs. Harlan Pyle/from
    N. C. Wyeth
"The Great West That Was," by Col. William F. Cody
*Hearst's Magazine,* September 1916
Courtesy of Andrew Wyeth

SITTING UP CROSS-LEGGED, WITH EACH HAND
    HOLDING A GUN . . .
Oil on canvas, h:37, w:26
Signed lower right: N. C. Wyeth 1906
"Bar 20 Range Yarns," by Clarence Edward Mulford
*The Outing Magazine,* May 1906
Courtesy of Alexander F. Treadwell

through May 1930, was also handsomely illustrated by N. C. Wyeth.

Once, when asked why he had given up the comforts of home and friends to travel into the West, to sleep on the ground or in the Indian hogan, to battle the heat of the desert or the icy cold of the mountains, Wyeth replied, after some reflection:

> Every man, whether he is an artist or not, has what is commonly called a soul. Sooner or later he yearns to express his soul in some way. He may start out in search of the unusual, the novel or the bizarre, and if he is an artist, he may find certain satisfaction in the theatrical—the great western plains, for instance, where you see a speck on the horizon, and have to travel all day to reach it or you see a mountain that looks a few hours journey off, and you ride three days to get to it. You may have the greatest sympathy for the people you meet, for the picturesqueness of their life and their traditions and clothing—but the time comes when his soul gets restless, and he finds that he has been enjoying a show in which he really has no fundamental part.
>
> He finds that in order to express himself fully, he has got to come back to the soil he was born on, no matter where it is—it may be the glorious White Mountains of New Hampshire, or the woods of Needham—the call is imperative, he has got to answer it. There is something in his bones that comes right out of the soil he grew up on—something that gives him a power and contract communion with life which no other place gives him.[3]

THE MYSTERY TREE
Oil on canvas, h:35½, w:25½
Signed lower left: N. C. Wyeth '08
*Reminiscences of a Ranchman,* by Edgar Beecher Bronson
George H. Doran Company, New York, 1910
Courtesy of J. N. Bartfield Art Galleries, Inc., New York

THE WAR CLOUDS
*Scribner's Magazine* (frontispiece), March 1909

THE HUNTER

THE SOLITUDE SERIES
*The Outing Magazine,* June 1907

THE MAGIC POOL

# 4

# *The Indian in His Solitude*

THE American Indian—what images the phrase conjures up! It brings to mind those brilliant horsemen of the Plains, the Cheyenne; the Sioux warrior chief resplendent in his magnificent warbonnet; the Apache, scourge of the Southwest, lurking in his stronghold amid the rocks and cactus of his desert country. These and more automatically come into mental focus at the mere mention of the phrase, for to most of us the Indians who figured so prominently in the young nation's push westward personify that colorful era, which in reality was not so very far in the past.

To N. C. Wyeth, however, the American Indian he found of greatest interest was the Indian of longer ago, the Indian faced by our forefathers when they first came to this land to settle. He was the Iroquois, the Huron, the Mohawk, and the Seneca. He was not the Indian of the vast plains, the mountains, or the desert. He was the Indian of poetry—the Woodland Indian of the Northeast.

As ferocious as his counterpart in the Far West, the Woodland Indian fought with as much dedication to preserve his land and the way of life that was rightfully his. The forces of nature played a major role in determining his every act, and in painting him Wyeth took account of that fact. With deep feeling and sensitive understanding, he depicted the Woodland In-

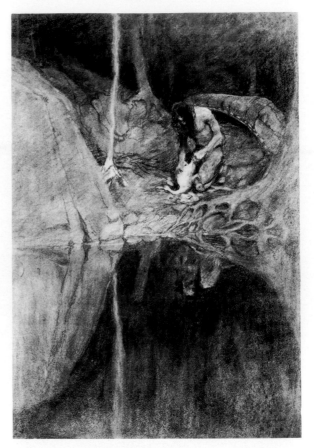

THE MOOSE CALL
*Scribner's Magazine,* October 1906

Preliminary Study for *The Indian in His Solitude*
Charcoal on paper, h:25½, w:16¼
Signed lower right: N.C.W. 1906
Collection of Douglas Allen, Jr.

dian, not as the gaudily painted warrior bent on massacre, but as a child of nature, whose moods dictated his day-to-day existence from birth to death.

In 1904, while studying at the Howard Pyle School, Wyeth painted one of the most popular of his Indian canvases, *The Moose Call,* which was subsequently reproduced in *Scribner's Magazine,* October 1906. To coincide with its appearance in the magazine, Scribner's also published the picture as a mounted print, which met with immediate success. It signaled Wyeth's emergence as one of America's foremost painters of nature and the unspoiled wilderness.

During 1906, Wyeth painted a number of other pictures of the Woodland Indian. Five of these appeared in the June 1907 issue of the old *Outing Magazine,* reproduced in full color with the title *The Indian in His Solitude.* They represent some of his finest work. Soon afterward, the magazine advertised that *The Indian in His Solitude* series was available as color prints, each measuring twelve by sixteen inches, mounted on heavy board and enclosed in an attractive box. Although this advertisement appeared regularly over a span of years, one mys-

tery remains. Our long-term research into the work of American illustrators brought to light only one complete set of the "Solitude" series and one single print.

Again in *Scribner's Magazine,* October 1907, the tranquil *Silent Fisherman* appeared. Painted in 1906, it may originally have been intended for the *Solitude* series, for it clearly interprets the feeling of solitude, showing the silent water and an Indian alone in contemplation. Some two years later, Wyeth made a series of four Indian paintings for *Scribner's Magazine.* These were reproduced in the December 1909 issue, to accompany a group of poems—"The Moods"—dedicated to the four seasons, written by George T. Marsh. This group of pictures served as the theme for what was to be Wyeth's first venture into the field of mural painting, in 1911: four decorative panels for the new Hotel Utica.

Perhaps one of the most beautiful portrayals of the Woodland Indian ever painted was Wyeth's *A Primitive Spearman. Scribner's,* always eager to provide their subscribers with the best in art and illustration, reproduced this painting as the frontispiece in October 1913 issue.

THE SILENT FISHERMAN (*The Lone Fisherman*)
*Scribner's Magazine* (frontispiece), October 1907

HIAWATHA'S FISHING
*The Children's Longfellow*
Houghton Mifflin Company, Boston, 1908

# A WYETH PORTFOLIO

## THE BEST OPPORTUNITY

### EVER OFFERED DISCERNING PEOPLE TO DECORATE THE HOME, DEN, OR CLUB WITH CHOICE PICTURES BY A MASTER PAINTER

It is not going too far to say that N. C. Wyeth is to-day one of our greatest, if not our *greatest* painter of American outdoor life. It is Wyeth's faculty of getting at "the soul of things" that makes his art so appealing.

#### The Solitude Series

the title of the five pictures in this Portfolio, is a series of canvases depicting the American Indian in his native haunts, surrounded by the all-pervading mystery of Nature. It is the Indian as he was, owner of this vast land, that has interested Wyeth so keenly.

The bigness of the outdoors, the forests, the plains, the *vastness of things*—all these qualities are found in these wonderful pictures; and, too, besides the "spirit," there is a masterly draughtsmanship throughout—and marvelous color harmonies. The whole set is a thing of beauty and singular charm.

#### The Color Work

in the reproduction of these pictures has been studiously followed. Every tone, every mass of brilliancy has been faithfully adhered to. The small black and white cuts herewith shown can give the purchaser only an idea of the subject matter treated.

#### The Size

The color reproduction of this Portfolio measures 12 by 16 inches. Each picture is mounted on heavy boards (ready for framing), making them about 17 by 22 inches over all. The set of five subjects is enclosed in an attractive box.

#### The Price

of these Portfolios is $4.50. Purchased singly, each picture costs $1.00. As a holiday item they would be welcomed as a choice and precious gift. For wall decoration of the Home, the Den, the Club, they are incomparable.

#### We Have Reserved

a few sets of this beautiful work to be used for Subscription purposes in connection with *The Outing Magazine*. This offer is open to both new and old Subscribers. While the limited number lasts, we will furnish one of the portfolios with every year's subscription to *The Outing Magazine* for $6.00.

##### NOTE THESE FIGURES

Year's Subscription to The Outing Magazine $3.00
A Wyeth Portfolio (five works of art) - 4.50
Total $7.50

YOU CAN OBTAIN ALL THIS FOR **$6**.00

Send in your subscription **NOW**

The supply of Portfolios is absolutely limited

## THE OUTING MAGAZINE

## SUBSCRIPTION DEPT., DEPOSIT, N. Y.

1907 Advertisement of *The Outing Magazine* for Wyeth's Solitude Series portfolio.

THE SPEARMAN

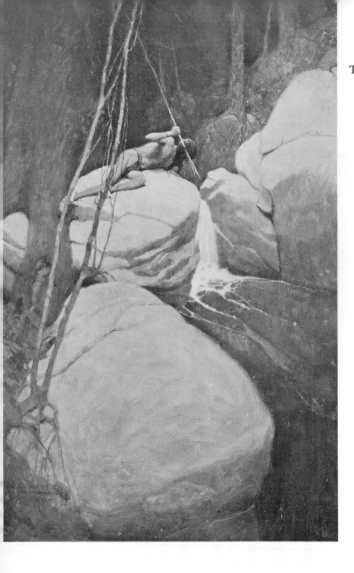

IN THE CRYSTAL DEPTHS

[ 60 ]

THE SILENT BURIAL

WINTER
Oil on canvas, h:33, w:30
Signed lower left: N. C. Wyeth '09
"The Moods," by George T. Marsh
*Scribner's Magazine,* December 1909
Courtesy of Andrew Wyeth

SPRING

SUMMER

AUTUMN

THE MOODS
*Scribner's Magazine,* December 1909

A PRIMITIVE SPEARMAN
*Scribner's Magazine* (frontispiece), October 1913

# 5

# *Brandywine Country*

Newell Convers Wyeth and Carolyn B. Bockius were married in April of 1906. At first they lived in Wilmington, as Wyeth continued to study under Howard Pyle and concentrated on fulfilling the many commitments that were coming his way. But, in the latter part of 1907, their first child was born, and they both felt that a family should be brought up in the country.

In seeking a satisfactory location for a permanent home, the young couple concentrated their attention on the rural area of Chadds Ford, Pennsylvania, which was a relatively short distance from Wilmington proper. They knew the area well, since Howard Pyle's summer home was there and for a number of years his art school held classes there during the warm summer months.

Wyeth was enamored of this Brandywine countryside with its rolling fields and wooded hillsides, its streams and its meadows and its farms. He loved its historical associations and its serenity. It reminded him of the country surrounding Needham, Massachusetts, where he was born and raised.

In the spring of 1908 the Wyeths moved to this Brandywine countryside and there they remained.

He once explained during an interview:

In me has revived a stronger and more vital interest and love for the life that lies about me. I am finding deeper pleasure, deeper meanings in the simple things in the country life here. Being older and more mature, I am realizing that one must go

MOWING
Oil on canvas, h:37½, w:27
Signed lower right: N. C. Wyeth, Chadds Ford, Pa.
Courtesy of Mr. & Mrs. Andrew Wyeth

beneath the surface to paint and so it is that my real loves, my real affections are reviving.[1]

In the spring of 1907 *Scribner's* had forwarded to Wyeth a copy of a poem entitled "Back to the Farm," by Martha Gilbert Dickinson Bianchi. He was so taken with the prospects it offered for picture material that he vowed he would spend the summer working on illustrations for it. His first was a delightful portrayal of a young girl holding a pitcher while a youthful scyther drank deep, for the work had been hard and the sun burned down on the landscape with a scorching heat. The painting, *Mowing,* won praise from all Wyeth's friends who saw it and a special commendation from Howard Pyle. This picture was not published in the series that appeared in *Scribner's Magazine,* August 1908. Another of similar theme took its place, but it is reproduced here along with the four that subsequently accompanied the poem, for which he also made eight charming pen-and-ink drawings.

N. C. Wyeth at work on a landscape, Chadds Ford, 1909

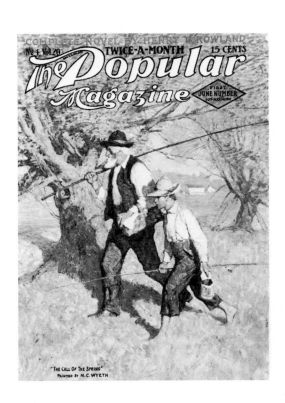

THE SCYTHERS (*Down in the hayfield where scythes glint through the clover . . .*)
Oil on canvas, h:37½, w:26¾
Signed lower right: N. C. Wyeth
"Back to the Farm," by Martha Gilbert Dickenson Bianchi
*Scribner's Magazine*, August 1908
Courtesy of University of Arizona Museum of Art, Samuel L. Kingan Collection

DOBBIN *(Plowing the Cornfield)*
Oil on canvas, h:37, w:28
Signed lower right: To my Chadds Ford/friend/Tinker
    Quimby/N. C. Wyeth/1907
"Back to the Farm," by Martha Gilbert Dickenson Bianchi
*Scribner's Magazine,* August 1908
Courtesy of Mrs. Sidney Ashcraft

Cover Illustration
*The Popular Magazine*, November 1913

Wyeth thrived in the Chadds Ford atmosphere. When not at work in his studio he could now often be seen somewhere about the acres of his farm discussing cabbages or cattle with his neighbors, or swinging an ax or following a plow with the best. He was absorbed in his community, his farm, and his family. Retreating to some isolated workshop had no place in Wyeth's scheme of things. He found inspiration in his contact with the life about him, and he began to paint more of the rural scene. It was no accident that much of his finest work should result from this theme.

N. C. Wyeth in his apple orchard at Chadds Ford, ca. 1944.
Photograph by William E. Phelps.
Courtesy of Mrs. N. C. Wyeth

My brothers and I were brought up on a farm and from the time I could walk I was conscripted into doing every conceivable chore that there was to do about the place. This early training gave me a vivid appreciation of the part the body played in action.

Now, when I paint a figure on horseback, a man plowing, or a woman buffeted by the wind, I have an acute bodily sense of the muscle-strain, the feeling of the hickory handle, or the protective bend of the head or squint of eye that each pose involves. After painting action scenes I have ached for hours because of having put myself in the other fellow's shoes as I realized him on the canvas.[2]

Pen-and-ink Drawings
*Susanna and Sue,* by Kate Douglas Wiggin
Houghton Mifflin Company, Boston, 1909

BRINGING HOME THE PUMPKINS
Oil on canvas, h:38, w:27
Signed lower right: N. C. Wyeth '07
"Back to the Farm," by Martha Gilbert Dickinson Bianchi
*Scribner's Magazine,* August 1908
Courtesy of Mr. and Mrs. Curtis Hutchins

CORN HARVEST IN THE HILL COUNTRY
*The Progressive Farmer,* October 1945

TWO BOYS IN A PUNT
Oil on canvas, h:37, w:26
Signed lower left: N. C. Wyeth
*The Popular Magazine* (cover),
August 7, 1915
Courtesy of Dr. & Mrs. William
A. Morton, Jr.

With the appearance of the illustrations for "Back to the Farm," other publishers took notice of his ability at portraying the rural scene. Soon he was busy making a series of delightful pen-and-ink drawings for a book called *Susanna and Sue* by Kate Douglas Wiggin, which appeared late in 1909.

Wyeth's versatility made it possible for him to turn to almost any subject or theme for his work, but his love of country life and the rural landscape remained apparent in many of his paintings for the rest of his life. The rural scenes that he did for periodicals were usually cover illustrations; they were made primarily for *The Popular Magazine, Progressive Farmer,* and *Country Gentleman.* But he painted many purely for pleasure and relaxation; these are reproduced in Chapter 11.

[ 71 ]

WHEN HE COMES HE WILL RULE OVER THE
    WHOLE WORLD
"The Lost Boy," by Henry Van Dyke
*Harper's Monthly Magazine,* December 1913

COME LIVE WITH US, FOR I THINK THOU ART
    CHOSEN
"The Lost Boy," by Henry Van Dyke
*Harper's Monthly Magazine,* December 1913

THE CHILD
*The Parables of Jesus* (frontispiece), by S. Parkes Cadman
David McKay Company, 1931

THE PARABLE OF THE LEAVEN
*The Parables of Jesus,* by S. Parkes Cadman
David McKay Company, 1931

THE BOY CHRIST IN THE CARPENTER'S SHOP
"The Man Nobody Knows," by Bruce Barton
*Woman's Home Companion,* December 1924

# 6

# *Religious Painting*

A sign on the door of N. C. Wyeth's studio read: "I will not have Good Fortune or God's Blessing let in while I am working."

"But," he once cheerfully remarked during an interview, "it doesn't seem to work because people just say they are neither Good Fortune or God's Blessing, and they walk right in."[1]

Wyeth seems to have attempted no paintings on biblical themes before 1912. That year, in the December issue of *Scribner's Magazine,* a story by Thomas Nelson Page, "The Stable of the Inn," was illustrated by two Wyeth paintings in color, and Wyeth paintings based on biblical stories were to appear from time to time in the years that followed.

On December 25, 1923, the Unitarian Laymen's League, which had headquarters in Boston, Massachusetts, held a private showing of the first six paintings Wyeth had completed for them based on the parables of Jesus. Approximately three years before then, this Unitarian group had decided the best way to engrave the parables indelibly on the minds of children and thus make their truths a lasting influence

would be to publish them in book form, without comment or moralizing, but illustrated with imagination, sympathy, skill, and beauty. Research indicated that in all the history of art, no serious attempt had ever been made to illustrate the parables as a whole. As the possibilities were studied, the committee became more and more convinced of the merit of the idea. They felt certain that such a book would have great appeal for, as well as an unconscious influence on, not only children but all who love beauty of picture and thought. Of course, the success of the project would depend almost entirely on their securing an artist possessed of the necessary talent and vision, one who would interpret the parables unawed by orthodox opinion and portray the characters in all their native virility, uninfluenced by the conventional ascetic precedents of religious art.

The search was ended when they found such a man in N. C. Wyeth.

A commission of this kind appealed to Wyeth as an opportunity to create true masterpieces. Undertaking the task in that spirit, he

MUHAMMAD THE PROPHET
Oil on canvas, h:47, w:38
Unsigned
"The Red Star," by Arthur Conan Doyle
*Scribner's Magazine,* January 1911
Collection of Douglas Allen, Jr.

devoted a year to preliminary study before he began the paintings. He himself said of his interpretations:

> The vitality of artistic expression is essentially auto-biographical. The creation of a picture, a poem, a musical composition, is a record of the artist's emotional and spiritual reaction to life and its traditions. This is true, whether the senses deal with beauty in the abstract or with the tangible drama and poetry of everyday existence. There is also that stimulating and valuable spirit of protest which is inevitably a factor in the agitation toward personal expression —the protest against unsatisfying existing standards or of tradition.
>
> This spirit of protest was in a considerable measure responsible for my interest in the painting of a series of paintings to ac-

company certain of the parables of Jesus— a protest against the inanities of teaching in the Sunday School classroom as I knew it.

From earliest boyhood the attendance at Sunday School was an unutterable bore to me. Only the inherited sense of duty, fostered carefully by my father and mother, made my attendance record respectable.

The years have passed and I have often looked back upon those tedious hours and have wondered at their barrenness. Now that I am able to read the Bible with almost the same excited interest with which I can read Homer, Shakespeare or Tolstoy, I begin to perceive some of the reasons why my Sunday School experiences were all but meaningless, and why they well nigh turned me away from the Bible forever for enjoyable and profitable reading.

The stories of the Bible were invariably

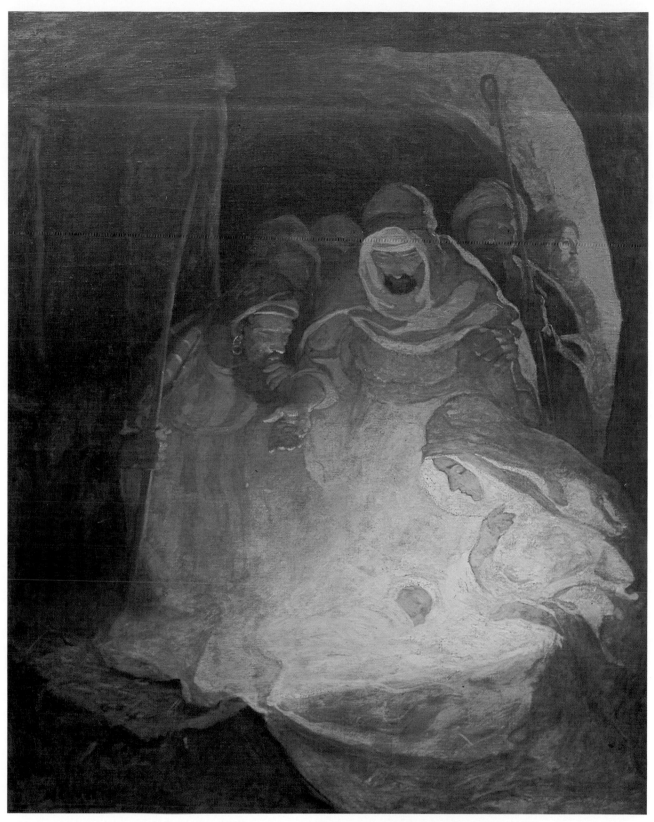

THE NATIVITY
Oil on canvas, h:47, w:38
Signed lower right: N. C. Wyeth
"The Stable of the Inn," by Thomas Nelson Page
*Scribner's Magazine*, December 1912
Collection of Douglas Allen, Jr.

THE PARABLE OF THE NET
*The Parables of Jesus,* by S. Parkes Cadman
David McKay Company, 1931

THE PARABLE OF THE SEED
*The Parables of Jesus,* by S. Parkes Cadman
David McKay Company, 1931

used as a bludgeon to drive home a moral lesson. In the process, all traces of those transcendent qualities of dramatic story telling and vivid beauty were lost. The inevitable harangue on the ethical deductions left me in a state of mental lethargy.

Art can become invaluable propaganda, but propaganda can never become art. Revealing the dramatic power and great beauty of a story from the Bible to the young mind is the surest method of releasing its moral and ethical force. Its potentiality for good must dawn upon the youth of its own power. It is the supreme art in the parables of Christ that is most valuable. The hordes of reformers and preachers since His day have done these allegories incalculable damage by turning them into cold doctrines of conduct. To preclude art with ethics is to rob it of life.

Referring particularly to the parables, let us recognize that an outstanding dramatic feature of these symbolisms is that they deal with the common, everyday life as seen by the Master. It is as though, while preaching, He raised His eyes to the hills and saw the Harvesters at work—the spontaneous parable of The Secret Growth of the Seed came to Him. As he talked to the multitude by the shore, He glimpsed the fishermen of Galilee and the parable of The Net was born. In passing through the sunlit streets of a Judean town He saw a mother at her task of bread making—and so came The Leaven.

Not once does He refer to the legends of ancient times or remote peoples. His source of inspiration was life, life as He saw and felt it about Him.

Is it not this spirit of the magnificent romance of reality which we must cherish when we attempt to reveal His teachings? Is this not a proper feature for an artist to emphasize when presuming to place a pictorial accompaniment to His marvelous words? Not pictures which attempt to interpret or explain, but rather conceptions which become as it were an obbligato to the magical singing melody of His stories.[2]

THE LOST LAMB
Oil on canvas, h:45, w:40
Signed lower right: N. C. Wyeth
Courtesy of Colby Art Museum,
Waterville, Maine

The original plan to have the parables published in book form did not work out. Instead, a committee made up of various religious denominations promoted the paintings as Christmas cards, which were printed in twelve colors and gold. Six hundred thousand were printed and sold at fifteen cents each. There was no financial gain for anyone, but a new standard was set in the quality of Christmas cards. These cards are now rare collector's items.

Eventually, the parable paintings Wyeth had done for the Unitarian Laymen's League did appear in a book—S. Parkes Cadman's *The Parables of Jesus*, which was published in 1931. By that time, another group of Wyeth's religious paintings had already been published. He had made these to illustrate Bruce Barton's *Children of the Bible*. They appeared in all issues of *Good Housekeeping* for the year 1929. But the crowning glory of his efforts in the field of religious painting must surely be the triptych housed in the National Cathedral in Washington, D.C. This is pictured in Chapter 11—"Murals, Lunettes, and the Triptych."

CAPTAIN BILL BONES (*All day he hung round the cove,*
   *or upon the cliffs, with a brass telescope.*)
Oil on canvas, h:47, w:38
Signed lower left: N. C. Wyeth
*Treasure Island,* by Robert Louis Stevenson
Charles Scribner's Sons, 1911
Courtesy of Mrs. Brigham Britton

THE ASTROLOGER *(On the fourth day comes the astrolo-*
*ger from the crumbling old tower . . .)*
Oil on canvas, h:40, w:32
Signed lower right: N. C. Wyeth
*The Mysterious Stranger,* by Mark Twain
Harper & Brothers, Publishers, 1916
(Copyright 1916 by Harper & Row, Publishers, Inc.;
    renewed 1944 by Clara Clemens Gabrilowitsch.)
Courtesy of Diamond M Foundation, Snyder, Texas

# 7

# *The Classics*

As I contemplated the writing of this chapter, my mind went back to my childhood. When I was ten or twelve years old, I often received books as gifts on birthdays, at Christmas, or sometimes on occasions that marked no special celebration in my young life. Those closest to me, aware of what an avid reader I was, did not have to ponder long over the choice of a gift that would please me.

The name N. C. Wyeth did not mean anything to me in those years. The pictures that were a part of these books did. The images of them remained with me and were more vivid in my memory, I daresay, than the spellbinding stories they illustrated.

But now I do know of N. C. Wyeth, and I recognize what his art has meant to me. I can now look at his contribution in perspective, and it is a certainty that what he gave to me he also gave to tens of thousands of others.

Most of the Wyeth-illustrated classics were published nearly a half century ago, but they are still being printed and still being bought as gifts for children, who some forty years hence will recall them as I have done. The cycle repeats itself—the long parade of beloved characters portrayed in story and illustration goes on and on in a never-ending procession.

In 1911, Robert Louis Stevenson's unforgettable *Treasure Island* was issued by Charles Scribner's Sons as the first book in its series known as the Scribner Illustrated Classics. For N. C. Wyeth, it marked the beginning of a long list of great books that he would be commissioned to illustrate over the next thirty years. His *Treasure Island* paintings had such dynamic storytelling quality that they must surely be ranked with the story itself—a classic marriage of text and pictures, for all time. His skill in projection—the heroic quality, rich color, and

CAPTAIN BONES ROUTS BLACK DOG
Oil on canvas, h:47, w:38
Signed lower right: N. C. Wyeth
*Treasure Island,* by Robert Louis Stevenson
Charles Scribner's Sons, 1911
Courtesy of Mr. and Mrs. John W. McCoy II

convincing interpretations in his paintings—made the characters living, breathing people who had really existed in the past. That Wyeth was able to do this was not strange. He had been subjected to Howard Pyle's theory of projection until it had become part of his very fiber.

In my own life I try to live the life that I depict. Some may wonder how I can live the life of the 12th century, which most of my costumed romance represents. All I can say is that the elemental feelings of long ago are identical with our own. The costumes and accessories of the 12th century may be different, but the sunlight on a bronzed face, the winds that blow across the marshlands, the moon illuminating the old hamlets of medieval England, the rain-soaked travelers of King Arthur's day passing across the moors are strictly contemporaneous in feeling. The farmer swinging a scythe uses the same muscles, experiences the same sensations as we do today. But you've got to do these things to understand them.[1]

The success of *Treasure Island* as a publishing enterprise was so great, and so lavish were the praises for the illustrations that con-

OLD PEW
Oil on canvas, h:47, w:38
Signed lower right: N. C. Wyeth 1911
*Treasure Island*, by Robert Louis Stevenson
Charles Scribner's Sons, 1911
Courtesy of Mrs. Andrew Wyeth

PREPARING FOR THE MUTINY *(Loaded pistols were*
*served out to all the sure men.)*
Oil on canvas, h:47, w:38
Signed upper left: N. C. Wyeth
*Treasure Island,* by Robert Louis Stevenson
Charles Scribner's Sons, 1911
Courtesy of Andrew Wyeth

THE HOSTAGE (*For all the world, I was led like a dancing
  bear.*)
Oil on canvas, h:47, w:38
Signed lower right: N. C. Wyeth
*Treasure Island,* by Robert Louis Stevenson
Charles Scribner's Sons, 1911
Courtesy of Mrs. Brigham Britton

JIM HAWKINS LEAVES HOME
Oil on canvas, h:47, w:38
Signed lower left: N. C. Wyeth
*Treasure Island*, by Robert Louis Stevenson
Charles Scribner's Sons, 1911
Courtesy of Wilmington Y.M.C.A., Wilmington, Delaware

Exterior and interior views of the studio N. C. Wyeth
built after his success illustrating the first of the
Scribner Classics, *Treasure Island*. The studio was completed
at the end of 1911.
Courtesy of William Penn Memorial Museum, Harrisburg

tributed to its appeal, that it did not take the Scribner organization long to formulate plans for a second book. The choice was *Kidnapped*, another Stevenson tale. When approached about the contemplated edition, Wyeth replied:

Your letter this morning affected me greatly and I am delighted. I want you to know that I have the greatest hopes, and unless I outclass Treasure Island I want you to cancel the entire scheme. Will write regarding "Kidnapped" in a few days.[2]

*Kidnapped* was published in 1913, and although the illustrations that were done for it did not "outclass" those done for *Treasure Island*, they stood on their own merit, as did those illustrating two more Stevenson stories that were later added to the shelf of Scribner Classics—*The Black Arrow* (1916) and *David Balfour* (1924).

His outstanding work for the series of Scribner Classics inevitably led to commissions from other publishers for illustrating juvenile books, and he threw himself wholeheartedly into all such assignments. A notable example was

MR. BALFOUR OF THE
HOUSE OF SHAWS
*Kidnapped,* by Robert Louis
Stevenson
Charles Scribner's Sons, 1913

Mark Twain's *The Mysterious Stranger,* which he illustrated for Harper's. Others, later, included *Robin Hood* and *Rip Van Winkle,* both for David McKay, *Robinson Crusoe* and *The White Company* for the Cosmopolitan Book Corporation, and the romantic *The Courtship of Miles Standish* for Houghton Mifflin. But the wonderful Scribner Classics went on and on too. For *The Boy's King Arthur,* he made an exciting, colorful series of pictures. The range of his interpretations continued to be varied and powerful.

Wyeth also occasionally became involved in writing the foreword or preface for a book, or in the actual choice of a title to become a part of the Scribner Illustrated Classics series.

In making the fourteen beautiful color illustrations for Jules Verne's *The Mysterious Island,* N. C. Wyeth realized one of his dearest wishes. The idea of this edition was his own. When the question came up of what book should follow in the series of illustrated books for young readers, he proposed *The Mysterious Island*, a favorite book of his, one he had always wished to illustrate.[3]

His reaction was sometimes unpredictable, though. When asked a few years later to illustrate another book by Jules Verne, *Twenty Thousand Leagues Under the Sea*, he flatly turned it down:

I positively cannot get up the least interest in Twenty Thousand Leagues etc. I have read it twice with all the concentration I am capable of and the damn thing sickens me. . . . I find so little in it which offers itself as a sympathetic vehicle on which to carry the things I love most to express.

If on the other hand you will consider another title for me I would be made very happy if the volume of patriotic verse were to be considered again. I had made up my mind and heart on that.[4]

BEN GUNN (*I saw a figure leap with great rapidity behind the trunk of a pine . . .*)
Oil on canvas, h:47, w:38
Signed lower right: N. C. Wyeth
*Treasure Island*, by Robert Louis Stevenson
Charles Scribner's Sons, 1911
Courtesy of Mrs. Andrew Wyeth

ON THE ISLE OF ERRAID (. . . *as long as the light lasted I kept a bright look-out . . .*)
Oil on canvas, h:40, w:32
Signed lower right: N. C. Wyeth
*Kidnapped*, by Robert Louis Stevenson
Charles Scribner's Sons, 1913
Courtesy of Mr. & Mrs. William V. Sipple, Jr.

AND LAWLESS, KEEPING HALF A STEP IN FRONT
OF HIS COMPANION . . . STUDIED OUT THEIR
PATH
*The Black Arrow,* by Robert Louis Stevenson
Copyright 1916 Charles Scribner's Sons;
renewal copyright 1944 N. C. Wyeth

This volume of patriotic poems was published in 1922—*Poems of American Patriotism* by Brander Matthews.

The first American classic to be undertaken for the Scribner series was James Fenimore Cooper's *The Last of the Mohicans*. Although it did not make its appearance until 1919, the planning for it went as far back as 1915. In a letter from Wyeth to Scribner's under the date April 16, 1915, he agreed to illustrate the book, and in a later letter he remarked:

> I got some remarkable material in the Lake George country. Cooked my supper over a fire in "Cooper's Cave" in spite of the fact that it is right in the heart of the city of Glens Falls.
>
> Found a rifle ball at Fort George where they are just now excavating for a R-R siding. The bullet is sponsor for one good picture idea at least.[5]

His apparent enthusiasm for illustrating *The Last of the Mohicans* turned to bitter disappointment when he received the proofs to review. In a letter to Mr. Scribner he complained:

> Your letter has in turn made me feel very miserable that I have misconstrued or made so much out of what was but a pleasant effort on your part to relieve my disappointment over the Cooper reproductions. No doubt I have been feeling the failure of the platemakers too bitterly, but it is hard, after four months of intense application, to see one's efforts reduced to such pitiable terms—and to know that they will be so multiplied.[6]

From this same letter it is clear that his pain was eased somewhat by the news of the choice of another book for him to illustrate, Charles Kingsley's *Westward Ho!*, and he conveyed his pleasure:

WE MUST BE IN THE DUNGEON . . .
*The Black Arrow*, by Robert Louis Stevenson
Copyright 1916 Charles Scribner's Sons;
renewal copyright 1944 N. C. Wyeth

THE BLACK ARROW FLIETH NEVERMORE
Oil on canvas, h:40, w:32
Signed upper right: N. C. Wyeth
*The Black Arrow*, by Robert Louis Stevenson
Copyright 1916 Charles Scribner's Sons;
renewal copyright 1944 N. C. Wyeth
Courtesy of Mr. Andrew Wyeth

[ 91 ]

E SIEGE OF THE ROUND-HOUSE (. . . *with a rush
of feet and a roar . . .*)
on canvas, h:40, w:32
ned lower right: N. C. Wyeth
*napped*, by Robert Louis Stevenson
arles Scribner's Sons, 1913
rtesy of Mrs. Russell G. Colt

ROBIN AND HIS MOTHER GO TO NOTTINGHAM
FAIR
*Robin Hood,* by Paul Creswick
David McKay, Publisher, 1917

CAPTAIN NEMO
*The Mysterious Island,* by Jules Verne
Copyright 1918 Charles Scribner's Sons;
renewal copyright 1946 Carolyn B. Wyeth and
Charles Scribner's Sons

I am delighted, as you must realize, that you have decided upon "Westward Ho!" I began the reading and study of this magnificent story some six weeks ago so already I have it well in hand. The Naval Bureau of Navigation in Washington has agreed to furnish me with all data concerning ships of the period, which was the main stumbling block for me.[7]

During the period when he was making the illustrations for *Westward Ho!* other projects were also under way, among them the pictures for the aforementioned *Robinson Crusoe* for Cosmopolitan Book Corporation.

The Scribner organization was anxious to proceed with *Westward Ho!* and rather concerned at the delay in getting all the finished paintings. To their inquiries on the status of the work, Wyeth replied:

Let me say right away that I am speeding up on Westward Ho! and expect to beat July 10th as a delivery date.

I am sorry that there seems to be so much concern about my behavior in doing the two books and beg to say that no favorable discrimination has been shown in either case. I would like to say here that the preparation for Westward Ho! has required more than twice as much time and money than I ever spent before, entailing two trips to Massachusetts (Haverhill and Salem libraries), also Washington and Philadelphia. The obscurity of maritime detail of 1580 is amazing. . . . The general lack of data made me recast the scheme of subjects several times in order to meet the kind of thing I could do with reasonable accuracy.

Robinson Crusoe, except for two pictures, the first and last, has required no data whatsoever except the few details I am perfectly familiar with.

The above stated facts are all that have created any discrimination in delivery dates.[8]

This was followed by a letter dated June 14 (1920):

Every hour and every ounce of energy is being directed in getting the Westward

SIR MADOR'S SPEAR BRAKE ALL TO PIECES, BUT
   THE OTHER'S SPEAR HELD
*The Boy's King Arthur,* edited by Sidney Lanier
Copyright 1917 Charles Scribner's Sons;
renewal copyright 1945 N. C. Wyeth

[ 93 ]

ESELDORF WAS A PARADISE FOR US BOYS
Oil on canvas, h:40, w:32
Signed upper left: N. C. Wyeth
*The Mysterious Stranger,* by Mark Twain.
Harper & Brothers Publishers, 1916
(Copyright 1916 by Harper & Row, Publishers, Inc.;
renewed 1944 by Clara Clemens Gabrilowitsch.)
Courtesy of Mr. & Mrs. Peter Hurd

ROBIN HOOD AND THE MEN OF THE GREENWOOD
Oil on canvas, h:40, w:32
Signed lower left: N. C. Wyeth
*Robin Hood* (cover design), by Paul Creswick
David McKay, Publisher, 1917
Copyright permission, courtesy of David McKay Company, Inc.
Courtesy of The New York Public Library

Ho! drawings completed as early as possible. Everything else is being sacrificed to do this.[9]

And on July 19 (1920):

I am trembling to tell you this but it must be said—I have withdrawn one of the Westward Ho! pictures and am doing it over again. With the set completed, the drawing showing John Brimblecombe stood out as distinctively inferior to the rest and I could not let it go through. . . .

I have thoroughly enjoyed doing the book, every minute of it, and were it not for the matter of time would feel genuinely sorry to say finis.[10]

Three Wyeth-illustrated books, in fact, were published in 1920—in addition to *Westward Ho!* and *Robinson Crusoe, The Courtship of Miles Standish* also made its appearance. *Robinson*

*Crusoe* had always been a particular favorite of Wyeth's, and in his preface to the book he wrote:

The outstanding appeal of this fascinating romance to me personally is the remarkably sustained sensation one enjoys of Crusoe's contact with the elements—the sea and the sun, the night and the storms, the sand, rocks, vegetation and animal life. In few books can the reader breathe, live and move with his hero so intensely, so easily and so consistently throughout the narrative. In Robinson Crusoe we have it; here is a story that becomes history, history living and moving, carrying with it irresistibly the compelling motive of a lone man's conquest over what seems to be inexorable fate.[11]

The year 1921 saw the publication of two more books with handsome illustrations by N. C. Wyeth: *Rip Van Winkle* (by the McKay organization) and *The Scottish Chiefs*, which was the eighth Scribner Illustrated Classic he had done.

In midsummer of 1921 he wrote to Scribner's of the progress being made on *The Scottish Chiefs*:

By this time, without much doubt, you have three more of the "Scottish Chiefs" drawings. More will follow soon. I hope that these come somewhere near your expectations. I am trying to keep a greater freshness of color and spontaneity of rendering, and still present considerable detail.[12]

Shortly thereafter, the work for this book was completed:

As I wired you, the last illustration for "Scottish Chiefs" was shipped in the morning of Aug. 12th. The subject is one that has given me so much difficulty from the beginning—"The Battle of Stirling Castle". I believe I have got something at last—a picture which rings with a certain historic conviction, a quality which I felt was very necessary, in that particular subject.

With reasonably good color plates, this series should take its place with the best I have done.[13]

His obvious pleasure with the results he had achieved in the illustrations done for this book inspired him to contemplate doing a num-

ROBIN HOOD AND HIS COMPANIONS LEND AID
. . . FROM AMBUSH
Oil on canvas, h:40, w:32
Signed upper left: N. C. Wyeth
*Robin Hood,* by Paul Creswick
David McKay, Publisher, 1917
Copyright permission, courtesy of David McKay Company,
Inc.
Courtesy of The New York Public Library

THE BATTLE AT GLENS FALLS
Oil on canvas, h:40, w:32
Signed lower left: N. C. Wyeth
*The Last of the Mohicans,* by James Fenimore Cooper
Copyright 1919 Charles Scribner's Sons;
renewal copyright 1947 Carolyn B. Wyeth
Courtesy of Mrs. Russell G. Colt

THE THREE FRIENDS
*The White Company,* by A. Conan Doyle
Cosmopolitan Book Corporation, New York, 1922

ber of others that might fit into the Scribner series. A few days later he wrote to Joseph Chapin:

> What I want you to do now, in the course of the next three or four years, is to let me go to Scotland and gather material for a series of five or six of Scott's novels!!! following with an edition of Burns and another of James Hogg.[14]

It is not known whether any serious consideration was given to this suggestion. Suffice it to say that Wyeth did not illustrate a book by any of these three writers.

During most of the 1920s he was inundated with a constant demand for his creations, however. This was a period when his output of mural work was enormous; he also fulfilled a good many commissions for advertising art in addition to illustrating fourteen books and painting countless pictures for stories in periodicals —a prodigious volume of creative activity.

While Wyeth was working on the paintings for *The Odyssey of Homer* (Houghton Mifflin), Scribner's approached him about illustrating *Gulliver's Travels,* which they proposed to add to the Illustrated Classics series. He replied to them in June of that year (1929):

AND WHEN THEY CAME TO THE SWORD THE
    HAND HELD, KING ARTHUR TOOK IT UP . . .
Oil on canvas
Signed lower right: N. C. Wyeth
*The Boy's King Arthur,* edited by Sidney Lanier
Copyright 1917 Charles Scribner's Sons;
renewal copyright 1945 N. C. Wyeth
Courtesy of Jack Webb

ROBIN MEETS MAID MARIAN
Oil on canvas, h:40, w:32
Signed lower left: N. C. Wyeth
*Robin Hood,* by Paul Creswick
David McKay, Publisher, 1917
Copyright permission, courtesy of David McKay Company,
    Inc.
Courtesy of the New York Public Library

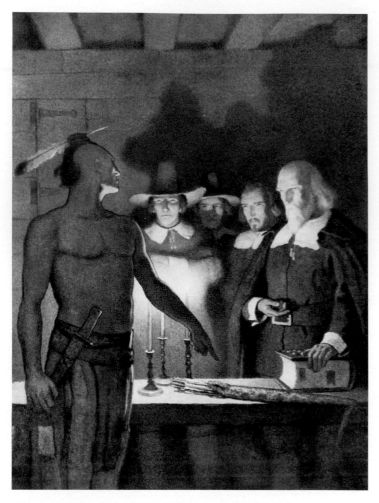

NEAR THEM WAS STANDING AN INDIAN, IN
ATTITUDE STERN AND DEFIANT
*The Courtship of Miles Standish,* by Henry Wadsworth
Longfellow
Houghton Mifflin Company, 1920

I am planning to take up Gulliver soon after I complete the Odyssey. This will be, I judge about the middle to the last of September. I am reading Gulliver now. . . .[15]

I am very tardy in acknowledging the receipt of the selected volume of Gulliver's Travels you sent to me. However, I am now prepared to report to you after a fresh reading and a reasonably careful study of the stories as material for illustration pictures.

Thirty years or more have passed since I last read the travels and it is significant to me that the first two parts remained vividly in my mind, whereas, the last parts left almost no impression at all. The voyage to

Laputa leaves me cold, but I do feel the urge to do a few amusing grotesqueries for Gulliver's visit to the Houyhnhnms.

It is a pity that we cannot get out an elaborately pictured volume of just the Lilliput and Brobdingnag adventures.[16]

The Scribner plans for *Gulliver* did not conform to Wyeth's ideas. He mulled over the proposal to do the book for several months, and on August 19, 1929, he wrote:

For reasons pertaining purely to my present state of artistic transition I wish to "beg off" and so postpone "Gulliver" for a year. I shall, of course, do nothing else in

WHY DON'T YOU SPEAK FOR YOURSELF, JOHN?
*The Courtship of Miles Standish,* by Henry Wadsworth
     Longfellow
Houghton Mifflin Company, 1920

KING MARK SLEW THE NOBLE KNIGHT SIR
TRISTRAM
Oil on canvas, h:40, w:32
Signed upper left: N. C. Wyeth
*The Boy's King Arthur,* edited by Sidney Lanier
Copyright 1917 Charles Scribner's Sons;
renewal copyright 1945 N. C. Wyeth
Courtesy of Mr. & Mrs. Ronald Rauch Randall

THE FIGHT IN THE FOREST
Oil on canvas, h:40, w:32
Signed lower right: N. C. Wyeth
*The Last of the Mohicans,* by James Fenimore Cooper
Copyright 1919 Charles Scribner's Sons;
renewal copyright 1947 Carolyn B. Wyeth
From the Permanent Collection, Brandywine River Museum

competitive book illustration in the meantime. . . .

I realize how much I am disturbing your plans, but no more so than a set of perfunctory drawings which would result were I forced to go through with the work. I have tried hard, ever since reading and planning the "Gulliver" series two months ago, to see my way clear to tackle them, but I cannot arouse sufficient spirit and enthusiasm.[17]

John Fox, Jr.'s *The Little Shepherd of Kingdom Come* was published by Scribner's as an Illustrated Classic in 1931, a handsome volume, particularly the elaborately printed and bound limited edition. It was the last book Wyeth was

HE WAS . . . SURPRISED AT THE SINGULARITY OF
    THE STRANGER'S APPEARANCE
*Rip Van Winkle,* by Washington Irving
David McKay, Publisher, 1921

THESE FOLKS WERE EVIDENTLY AMUSING
THEMSELVES . . .
*Rip Van Winkle*, by Washington Irving
David McKay, Publisher, 1921

JOHN OXENHAM
Oil on canvas, h:40, w:30
Signed upper left: N. C. Wyeth
*Westward Ho!*, by Charles Kingsley
Copyright 1920 Charles Scribner's Sons;
renewal copyright 1948 Carolyn B. Wyeth
Courtesy of George D. Beck

I STOOD LIKE ONE THUNDERSTRUCK . . .
Oil on canvas, h:40, w:30
Signed lower right: N. C. Wyeth
*Robinson Crusoe,* by Daniel Defoe
Cosmopolitan Book Corporation, 1920
Copyright permission, courtesy of David McKay Company,
    Inc.
Courtesy of Wilmington Institute & New Castle County
    Libraries, Wilmington, Delaware

KING EDWARD
*The Scottish Chiefs,* by Jane Porter
Copyright 1921 Charles Scribner's Sons;
renewal copyright 1949 Carolyn B. Wyeth

to illustrate for eight years. Then came Marjorie Kinnan Rawlings's delightful *The Yearling,* chosen as a Scribner Illustrated Classic in spite of the fact that it was a new book. To obtain authentic background material for his *Yearling* illustrations, Wyeth made a trip to Florida to study the locale firsthand:

I'm already quite saturated with the appearance of Baxter's Island clearing, the neighboring "sink" and the vast surrounding wilderness of palmetto scrub-lands.

This is a surprisingly wild country as you move back from the few main highways and the people who live on these endless sandy roads are as interesting and authentic types of American pioneers, hunters and trappers as I ever saw.

I've watched "gators" slide into the dark streams, caught a glimpse of a black bear and actually heard the scream of a panther last night. I was standing in one of those "bays" of live-oak and pines. There was a light wind which moved the Spanish

PAUL REVERE
*Poems of American Patriotism,* edited by Brander Matthews
Copyright 1922 Charles Scribner's Sons;
renewal copyright 1950

[ 111 ]

RIP VAN WINKLE (*It was with some difficulty that he found the way to his own house . . .*)
Oil on canvas, h:40, w:30
Signed lower left: N. C. Wyeth
*Rip Van Winkle,* by Washington Irving
David McKay Company, 1921

SIR NIGEL SUSTAINS ENGLAND'S HONOR IN TH
LISTS
Oil on canvas, h:40, w:30
Signed lower left: N. C. Wyeth
*The White Company,* by A. Conan Doyle
Cosmopolitan Book Corporation, 1922
Courtesy of Mrs. N. C. Wyeth

THE MIDNIGHT ENCOUNTER
*Legends of Charlemagne,* by Thomas Bulfinch
Cosmopolitan Book Corporation, 1924

THE WATER-HOLE
Oil on canvas, h:28, w:36
Signed lower left: N. C. Wyeth
*The Oregon Trail* (end papers), by Francis Parkman
Little, Brown & Company, 1925
Courtesy of Southern Arizona Bank & Trust Company, Tucson

moss back and forth spectrally, and through this the moon-light poured. The moving shadows made the ground we were standing on writhe and undulate as though it were actually alive. The distant fearful call of that cat added the last touch of blood-chilling accompaniment to the scene.[18]

In that same year, 1939, Little, Brown and Company issued an illustrated edition of Helen Hunt Jackson's celebrated *Ramona.* This was the last outstanding literary work for which Wyeth was to paint the illustrations.

Following is a list of the great masterpieces of writing to which N. C. Wyeth contributed the illustrations:

*Treasure Island* by Robert Louis Stevenson
Charles Scribner's Sons, 1911.

*Kidnapped* by Robert Louis Stevenson
Charles Scribner's Sons, 1913.

*The Black Arrow* by Robert Louis Stevenson
Charles Scribner's Sons, 1916.

*The Mysterious Stranger* by Mark Twain
Harper & Brothers, 1916.

*The Boy's King Arthur*
(Edited by) Sidney Lanier
Charles Scribner's Sons, 1917.

*Robin Hood* by Paul Creswick
David McKay, 1917.

*The Mysterious Island* by Jules Verne
Charles Scribner's Sons, 1918.

*The Last of the Mohicans*
by James Fenimore Cooper
Charles Scribner's Sons, 1919.

*Westward Ho!* by Charles Kingsley
Charles Scribner's Sons, 1920.

*Robinson Crusoe* by Daniel Defoe
Cosmopolitan Book Corporation, 1920.

THE DUEL
Oil on canvas, h:34, w:25
Signed upper left: N. C. Wyeth
*David Balfour,* by Robert Louis Stevenson
Copyright 1924 Charles Scribner's Sons;
renewal copyright 1952 Carolyn B. Wyeth and
    Charles Scribner's Sons
Courtesy of Alexander F. Treadwell

THE PARKMAN OUTFIT—HENRY CHATILLON, GUIDE
   AND HUNTER
Oil on canvas, h:40½, w:29⅛
Signed lower left: N. C. Wyeth
*The Oregon Trail*, by Francis Parkman
Little, Brown and Company, 1925
Courtesy of Southern Arizona Bank & Trust Company, Tucson

BUFFALO HUNT
Oil on canvas, h:40, w:30
Signed lower left: N. C. Wyeth
*The Oregon Trail,* by Francis Parkman
Little, Brown and Company, 1925
Courtesy of J. N. Bartfield Galleries, Inc., New York

EMERGING INTO AN OPENING . . .
Oil on canvas, h:40, w:32
Signed lower left: N. C. Wyeth/To Peter/from Grandfather
*The Deerslayer,* by James Fenimore Cooper
Copyright 1925 Charles Scribner's Sons;
renewal copyright 1953
Courtesy of Peter Wyeth Hurd

MELISSA
*The Little Shepherd of Kingdom Come,* by John Fox, Jr.
Copyright 1931 Charles Scribner's Sons;
renewal copyright © 1959

*The Courtship of Miles Standish*
   by Henry W. Longfellow
   Houghton Mifflin Company, 1920.

*The Scottish Chiefs* by Jane Porter
   Charles Scribner's Sons, 1921.

*Rip Van Winkle* by Washington Irving
   David McKay, 1921.

*Poems of American Patriotism*
   by Brander Matthews
   Charles Scribner's Sons, 1922.

*The White Company* by A. Conan Doyle
   Cosmopolitan Book Corporation, 1922.

*David Balfour* by Robert Louis Stevenson
   Charles Scribner's Sons, 1924.

*Legends of Charlemagne*
   by Thomas Bulfinch
   Cosmopolitan Book Corporation, 1924.

*The Deerslayer* by James Fenimore Cooper
   Charles Scribner's Sons, 1925.

THE FIGHT WITH OLD SLEWFOOT
*The Yearling*, by Marjorie Kinnan Rawlings
Copyright 1939 Charles Scribner's Sons;
renewal copyright © 1967

THE ROAD TO VIDALIA
Oil on canvas, h:48¼, w:39¼
Signed lower right: N. C. Wyeth
*Cease Firing*, by Mary Johnston
Houghton Mifflin Company, 1912
Courtesy of James B. Wyeth

8

# From Blackbeard to St. Nick

Iɴ presenting the many types of subject matter that N. C. Wyeth painted, his works have been arranged in specific categories. To have presented them in chronological order would have resulted in a disconcerting hodgepodge. Among his book and magazine illustrations, however, are a sizable number on widely varied themes that do not readily lend themselves to such categorizing. These are grouped together here—and this chapter could aptly have been titled "Miscellaneous Book and Magazine Illustration." As might be expected, though, there is nothing "miscellaneous" about their quality.

Most of these illustrations were originally made for magazines; many appeared later as book illustrations when the stories were reprinted in book form. The authors whose tales were made more vivid by Wyeth's pictorial skill were among the best known and most popular of the period: Peter B. Kyne, James B. Connolly, Arthur Conan Doyle, Dorothy Canfield Fisher, Edna Ferber, Ben Ames Williams, Bret Harte, Stewart Edward White, Rafael Sabatini, Harold Bell Wright, and James Oliver Curwood, to name only a few.

Nor can we ignore the dust wrapper illustrations Wyeth painted for Kenneth Roberts's historical novels—*Arundel, The Lively Lady,* and *Rabble in Arms*—or the exceptional illustrations done for his *Trending into Maine,* works so praiseworthy that several of them have been included in Chapter 11, which is devoted to his easel paintings.

The Wyeth Edition of the *Bounty* trilogy

THE FIRST CARGO
Oil on canvas, h:47, w:38
Signed lower left: N. C. Wyeth
"The First Cargo," by Arthur Conan Doyle
*Scribner's Magazine,* December 1910
Courtesy of The New York Public Library

brought together those three outstanding works by Nordhoff and Hall: *Mutiny on the Bounty, Men Against the Sea,* and *Pitcairn's Island.*

Last but not least were the Boston Blackie stories by none other than the great No. 6606.

Since this chapter concludes the presentation of N. C. Wyeth's work in the field of book and magazine illustration, which was certainly the field in which he was most renowned, it might be appropriate to consider briefly not only that period termed by many the Golden Age of American Illustration, but also Wyeth's personal feelings regarding his craft.

The Golden Age of American Illustration roughly covered some fifty years. Following the Civil War, the industrial revolution intensified in the United States, and with it came a phenomenal burgeoning of inventive genius. The printing industry was one of those most affected by the new developments. Practical inventions and vastly improved techniques resulted in making the printed word available to the general public more cheaply than ever before. This was especially true in the case of periodicals—their stories were supplemented by more illustrations than had been economically possible in the past. The change soon brought into prominence some of the names that became outstanding in American art and illustration—among them Winslow Homer, A. B. Frost, Edwin A. Abbey, Frederic Remington, and Howard Pyle. The best talents were commissioned by such topflight publishers as Harper's, Scribner's, and Century; the myriad of other publications that were appearing on the scene were forced to turn to the inferior ones. Even these lesser illustrators had little difficulty in getting their work accepted for publication, however, and the pages of both periodicals and books began to be filled with second-rate work.

It was for just this reason that Howard Pyle founded his courses of study in illustration at Drexel Institute and later at his own school in Wilmington. The young students who studied under him and a few of the established illustrators who came to him for guidance during the late eighteen nineties and early nineteen hundreds were, in a great measure, responsible for bringing a new quality to illustration for the remainder of the Golden Age. Of course the art of illustration did not survive only because of Howard Pyle and those who studied

MOOSE HUNTERS—A MOONLIT NIGHT
Oil on canvas, h:40, w:21½
Signed upper left: N. C. Wyeth
*Scribner's Magazine,* October 1912
Courtesy of Mr. & Mrs. Andrew Wyeth

FROM AN UPPER SNOW PLATFORM . . . A SECOND
MAN HEAVED THEM OVER THE BANK
"How They Opened the Snow Road," by W. M. Raine and
W. H. Eader
*The Outing Magazine,* January 1907

LONG HENRY DROVE CAUTIOUSLY ACROSS THE
SCENE OF YESTERDAY'S ACCIDENT
"How They Opened the Snow Road," by W. M. Raine
and W. H. Eader
*The Outing Magazine,* January 1907

THE EIGHT MINERS FOLLOWED THE
TREACHEROUS TRAIL
"How They Opened the Snow Road," by W. M. Raine and
W. H. Eader
*The Outing Magazine,* January 1907

HE . . . FLUNG THE SIX POUNDS OF POWERFUL
EXPLOSIVE OUT INTO THE GREAT SNOW
COMB
"How They Opened the Snow Road," by W. M. Raine and
W. H. Eader
*The Outing Magazine,* January 1907

THE DRIFTS BECAME HEAVIER
"A Christmas Venture," by S. Weir Mitchell
*Ladies' Home Journal,* December 1907

THE VEDETTE
Oil on canvas, h:48¼, w:38¼
Signed lower right: N. C. Wyeth '10
*The Long Roll,* by Mary Johnston
Houghton Mifflin Company, 1911
Courtesy of Mr. & Mrs. George A. Weymouth

under him. There were other great illustrators who had that special talent that enabled them to survive changes in taste and vogue. But there were many more who lacked that gift.

Like Howard Pyle, N. C. Wyeth was deeply disturbed as he contemplated the gradual deterioration of illustration as a result of the lack of sound basic training in the art schools. To be a success in the field of illustration it was not only essential that a student know how to draw, but, more important, that he be educated to project himself into the soul of the character to be depicted in an illustration. In this the teaching of young, aspiring illustrators was sadly lacking. Howard Pyle had been deeply aware of this fundamental, and he made it basic in the teaching of his own students. N. C. Wyeth had been thoroughly indoctrinated in this approach.

It is a universal opinion among discriminating readers that illustration in the majority of cases is a superimposed burden upon the story it pretends to illustrate. I am in hearty sympathy with that opinion. It is too often a detached art and makes little pretense to be in working harmony and sympathetically submissive to the spirit of the tale. In being submissive it will add

power and charm to the story but if it precludes the author's artistry by repeating in bald assertions the main incidents and characters it becomes a vital menace and detriment in the expression of any writing, be the writing ever so powerful and the pictures ever so inferior.

The artistic powers of an illustrator spring from the same source as do the powers of the painter; but the profound difference lies in the fact that the illustrator submits his inspiration to a definite end; the painter carries his into infinitude. Therefore, the work of the illustrator resolves itself into a craft and he must not lose sight of that very important factor.

To successfully illustrate he must be subjective. It is important business to use restraint, particularly in the choice of subjects. The ability to select subject matter is an art in itself and calls to action similar dramatic instincts required in the staging of

THE FRONTIERSMAN
Oil on canvas, h:33½, w:24½
Signed lower right: N. C. Wyeth
*The Popular Magazine* (cover), March 15, 1912
Courtesy of Mr. Russell B. Aitken

THE BATTLE
Oil on canvas, h:45¾, w:36¾
Signed lower right: N. C. Wyeth 1910
*The Long Roll,* by Mary Johnston
Houghton Mifflin Company, 1911
Courtesy of Mr. & Mrs. George A. Weymouth

a play. The illustrator must first feel the power of the story in all its rhythm and swing, at the same time sense just at the right moment to step in with his illustration just as the play producer endeavors to intensify and enhance the drama with his ingenious stage properties and effects. To do this requires an amount of instinctive ability, but, like everything else, it improves with experience and serious study.

By avoiding the shackles of explicit action and detail the illustrator will find a field of far greater range upon which to exercise his powers, emotional and technical, and is given a better chance to produce something of real merit.[1]

Convincing illustration must ring true to life. The characters should be of flesh and blood, not puppets who strike attitudes for the sake of composition, or manikins which serve as drapes for clothes, however effective the costumes in themselves may be.[2]

The time rapidly approached when the Golden Age of American Illustration began to come to an end. N. C. Wyeth had been a vital part of this age, and he became depressed by the changes. His thoughts turned more and more to mural painting. He also began to take on more commercial assignments. Although his output of book illustrations maintained a steady pace, his interest in purely magazine illustration took a sharp decline. In a letter to Joseph Chapin of Scribner's, dated November 11, 1919, he remarked:

GOLYER
*The Pike County Ballads,* by John Hay
Houghton Mifflin Company, 1912

LITTLE BREECHES
*The Pike County Ballads,* by John Hay
Houghton Mifflin Company, 1912

BOSTON BLACKIE FORCED DRAWER
AFTER DRAWER
"Boston Blackie Stories," by No. 6606
*The American Magazine,* July 1914

Headpiece Illustration
"The Quest of Narcisse LaBlanche," by George T. Marsh
*Scribner's Magazine,* May 1916

STONEWALL JACKSON
Oil on canvas, h:47, w:38¼
Signed lower right: N. C. Wyeth '10
*The Long Roll,* by Mary Johnston
Houghton Mifflin Company, 1911
Courtesy of Alexander F. Treadwell

Magazine illustration has become a very unsatisfactory job. The pay in most instances is liberal enough, but presentation to the public is rotten! One must needs work abortively to help the engraver, thus ruining the finer pleasure in making the pictures, and then one gets a bad reproduction anyway.[3]

Did Wyeth's attitude toward magazine illustration stem from emotions that may have prevailed generally at the time? Or had he

THE CARPETBAGGERS
Oil on canvas, h:49, w:39
Signed lower left: N. C. Wyeth
*The Pike County Ballads* (cover design), by John Hay
Houghton Mifflin Company, 1912
Courtesy of Diamond M Foundation, Snyder, Texas

JIM BLUDSOE OF THE PRAIRIE BELLE
Oil on canvas, h:32, w:24
Signed lower right: N. C. Wyeth
*The Pike County Ballads,* by John Hay
Houghton Mifflin Company, 1912
Courtesy of Diamond M Foundation, Snyder, Texas

THE OPIUM SMOKER (*"Finally I Became a Daily
       User of Opium"*)
Oil on canvas, h:32, w:44
Signed upper right: N. C. Wyeth 1913
"A Modern Opium Eater," by No. 6606
*The American Magazine,* June 1914
Courtesy of Mr. and Mrs. Dallett Hemphill

HE'D LET A ROAR OUTER HIM, AN' MEBBE HE'D
   SING, "HAIL COLUMBIA, HAPPY LAND!"
"The Rakish Brigantine," by James B. Connolly
*Scribner's Magazine*, August 1914

'N THERE'S A DRAGON BLACK AS INK WI' ONE EYE
Oil on canvas, h:44, w:32
Signed lower left: N. C. Wyeth
"The Rakish Brigantine," by James B. Connolly
*Scribner's Magazine*, August 1914
Courtesy of The Needham Public Library, Needham, Mass.

N. C. Wyeth posed with the
   completed illustrations for
"The Rakish Brigantine."
Courtesy of the Delaware
Art Museum

SONG OF THE EAGLE THAT MATES WITH THE
   STORM
Oil on canvas, h:40, w:32
Signed lower right: N. C. Wyeth
"The Wild Woman's Lullaby," by Constance Lindsay
   Skinner
*Scribner's Magazine,* December 1916
Courtesy of Thomas Gilcrease Institute, Tulsa, Oklahoma

OH, MORGAN'S MEN ARE OUT FOR YOU; AND
   BLACKBEARD—BUCCANEER!
"The Golden Galleon," by Paul Hervey Fox
*Scribner's Magazine,* August 1917

THE DEATH OF FINNWARD KEELFARER
Oil on canvas, h:44, w:32
Signed lower left: N. C. Wyeth
"The Waif Woman," by Robert Louis Stevenson
*Scribner's Magazine,* December 1914
Courtesy of Mr. & Mrs. Joseph E. Levine

simply stated a personal observation after careful consideration? The statistics are interesting. From that day in 1903 when his *Saturday Evening Post* cover appeared, to the end of 1919, a span of seventeen years, Wyeth contributed to approximately twenty-four different periodicals in 275 issues, making a total number of 561 illustrations for them. From 1920 through 1945,

an even longer span of time, the number of periodicals for which he worked dropped to nineteen; the number of issues to 100, which contained only 229 Wyeth illustrations.

In 1927 a series of articles was published about notable illustrators, and one of these was devoted to Wyeth:

THE FIGHT IN THE PEAKS
Oil on canvas
Signed lower left: N. C. Wyeth
*Scribner's Magazine*, February 1917
Courtesy of Mr. & Mrs. R. R. M. Carpenter, Jr.

FRONTIER TRAPPER
Oil on canvas, h:34, w:32
Signed lower right: N. C. Wyeth
Copyright by The Book House for Children, 1920; from
    *My Book House*
Courtesy of the United Educators, Inc.,
    Lake Bluff, Illinois

OLE ST. NICK (OLD KRIS)
Oil on canvas, h:41½, w:31
Signed lower right: N. C. Wyeth
*The Country Gentleman* (cover), December 1925
Courtesy of John Denys McCoy

COLUMBUS' LANDING
*Essentials of American History,* by
    Thomas Bonaventure Lawler
Copyright 1918 by Thomas Bonaventure Lawler; renewed
    1946 by T. Newman Lawler
Ginn and Company

A CALIFORNIA MISSION
Oil on canvas, h:39¼, w:26¼
Signed lower left: N. C. Wyeth
*Essentials of American History,* by
    Thomas Bonaventure Lawler
Copyright 1918 by Thomas Bonaventure Lawler; renewed
    1946 by T. Newman Lawler
Ginn and Company
Courtesy of Mr. & Mrs. Richard DeVictor

THE BOY COLUMBUS ON THE WHARF IN GENOA
*New Geography,* Book One, the Frye-Atwood Geographical
    Series
Copyright 1917 by Alexis Everett Frye; renewed 1945
    by Teresa A. Frye.
Ginn and Company

Cover Illustration
*Ladies' Home Journal,* March 1922
Courtesy of the *Ladies' Home Journal*

Unpublished Illustration
Oil on canvas, h:31¾, w:34
Signed upper right: N. C. Wyeth
Inscription lower right: To my friend Kamp from N.C.W.
Made for "Snake and Hawk," by Stephen Vincent
 Benét, a story that appeared in the *Ladies'*
 *Home Journal,* March 1923
Courtesy of Mr. & Mrs. Anton Kamp

BIG BLACK BEPPO AND LITTLE BLACK BEPPO
"Time and Tide," Adriana Spadoni
*Woman's Home Companion,* July 1924

Preliminary Study for "Sea-Fever"
Drawing on paper, h:13⅜, w:9⅝
Signed lower right: N C W
The finished illustration was used with John
 Masefield's "Sea-Fever"
*World of Music Series—Discovery*
Ginn & Company, 1938
Courtesy of Mr. & Mrs. Richard Layton

THERE WAS AN OLD WOMAN TOST UP IN A
 BASKET . . .
Oil on panel, h:36, w:26
Signed upper left: N. C. Wyeth
*Anthology of Children's Literature,* compiled by
 Edna Johnson and Carrie E. Scott
Houghton Mifflin Company, 1940
Courtesy of The Free Library of Philadelphia and
 Houghton Mifflin Company

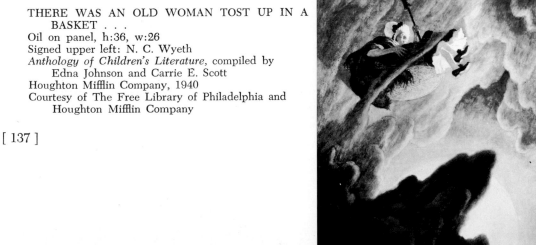

[ 137 ]

"PECULIARSOME" ABE
Oil on panel, h:32, w:24
Signed lower right: N. C. Wyeth
*Anthology of Children's Literature,*
   comp. by Edna Johnson
   and Carrie E. Scott
Houghton Mifflin Company, 1940
Courtesy of The Free Library of
   Philadelphia and Houghton
   Mifflin Company

Not long ago, there sat a gentleman before an open book. His manner was a sad manner. In his eye there was, perhaps, a tear.

"Where," he asked, "where is there another Howard Pyle?"

Tears are a great luxury. Likewise there is no other Howard Pyle. With him there passed a truly great illustrator. But illustration did not end there. There is, for in-

stance, N. C. Wyeth. And there are some sensations we experience in Wyeth illustration that few other illustrators can offer. I doubt if we find their exact counterpart in the illustration of Wyeth's principal teacher, Howard Pyle himself.

It is its own signature, and an inspiring one. There is a heroic treatment of anatomy, for example, that makes a Wyeth masculine-type so gloriously strong and virile,—you

SHE MAKES A GRAND LIGHT (*The Burning of the*
   Bounty)
Oil on panel, h:34, w:25
Signed lower right: N. C. Wyeth
*The Bounty Trilogy,* by Charles Nordhoff and James
   Norman Hall
Little, Brown and Company, 1940
Courtesy of The Free Library of Philadelphia
   and Little, Brown and Company

FIRST FARMER OF THE LAND
"The First Farmer of the Land,"
   by Donald Culross Peattie
*The Country Gentleman,* February 1946
(This illustration was on Wyeth's easel, in the
process of completion, at the time of his
fatal accident.)

[ 139 ]

ALLONS! . . . IT IS TIME TO MAKE AN END
"The Duel on the Beach," by Rafael Sabatini
*Ladies' Home Journal,* September 1931
Courtesy of the *Ladies' Home Journal*

look for a new discovery and technique. Then that romance of color, of wave, of cloud. Of those authentic, yet fascinating ships that toss or float over seas, fabulously stormy or credibly calm.

In the affections of the adolescent boy, there will be few to replace N. C. Wyeth. To the very human critic Wyeth has an insured niche. When one is wearied a bit it is a pleasant relaxation to rediscover the sheer color ecstasy and eternal decorative beauty of an illustration by N. C. Wyeth.[4]

That accolade is just as true today as when it was written.

UNION TROOPS BOARDING MISSISSIPPI
    RIVER STEAMERS
Oil on panel, h:19½, w:14½
Signed lower right: N. C. Wyeth
"The Peach-Brandy Leg,"
    by Mabel Thompson Rauch
*Woman's Day,* August 1945
Courtesy of Kennedy Galleries, Inc., New York

FIRST AID TO THE HUNGRY
Circa 1915 advertisement illustrated by N. C. Wyeth
Courtesy of the W. K. Kellogg Company

# 9 *Commercial Art*

EARLY in his career N. C. Wyeth learned that commissions for paintings to be used exclusively for advertising purposes were financially worthwhile. Following his first such assignment—for Cream of Wheat—commercial projects were offered to him in steadily increasing numbers: work for magazine advertisements, calendars, posters. He was highly sought after, and despite the large number of paintings he turned out for magazine and book illustration, his output of commercial artwork was considerable. In style, freshness, and appeal, most of his commercial creations are as alive today as they were some fifty years ago; they are not "dated," like the work of so many of the well-known commercial artists of that period.

The financial rewards of doing an abundance of commercial work were a temptation, but Wyeth was well aware of the pitfalls. His commitments for book and magazine illustration and his interest in mural painting and in improving his techniques in easel painting led him to explain his feelings to Joseph Chapin. In a letter dated November 11, 1919, he wrote:

In the meantime opportunities in the illustrating field have piled in beyond anything I ever experienced, particularly for the advertising houses. To date I have turned down all the latter with the exception of a single painting for the Winchester Rifle. In a sense it has been somewhat of an ordeal, for in several cases (three, to be accurate) the price has been 1500.00 for single drawings.

I believe that most of my friends, worthy to know this, would say, "How foolish!". To me it is not foolish, even though it may be impractical. Heaven knows! I've none too much idealism, and what little I've got must be applied. So it is that I am resolved not to be inundated with a character of work which is such an insidious antidote for the qualities within my nature which are struggling for expression. The miserable failure of the older men of my generation in illustration to advance to higher forms of artistic expression stands as an obvious and mighty lesson, and not to

NEW YEAR'S DAY

FOURTH OF JULY
Similar in content to the illustration Wyeth made
in 1904 for *The Delineator* (see Chapter 2).

THANKSGIVING I

CHRISTMAS DAY

BANK HOLIDAY POSTERS
(Commissioned by the United States Treasury Depart-
ment; published by The Canterbury Company, Inc.,
Chicago; copyrighted 1921 by Charles Daniel Frey
Company, New York and Chicago.)

make an effort to avoid their errors would be the height of weakness.

Advertising art has indeed progressed remarkably and on the whole is much more interesting to look at than the illustrated story section of most periodicals, but that does not justify it to the artist by any means, for the demands of the advertiser are far more confining and far more artificial than the demands of an author. The big prices offered are blinding and it is so damned easy not to see the danger.[1]

It is, of course, both impractical and impossible to reproduce here everything Wyeth did in the field of commercial art. Many of the originals have disappeared entirely; some doubtless remain in the hands of unknown owners. Others that might have been reproduced appeared originally in periodicals that used a very poor grade of paper and hence are not in good enough condition today to make satisfactory reproduction copy.

Wyeth's Cream of Wheat paintings were made in 1906 and 1907, but all were copyrighted 1907. They were frequently reproduced in the top periodicals for a number of years after their initial appearance. Originally, they were housed in the Minneapolis cereal plant of the National Biscuit Company; later they were donated to the Minneapolis Institute of Art. The painting *Alaska*, while being restored for presentation, was unfortunately destroyed by fire in 1969.

The calendar painting for Winchester Arms that Wyeth mentioned in his 1919 letter to his friend Chapin (*The Moose Hunters*) was not his only commission for that firm. He had painted another hunting scene for a Winchester Arms calendar in 1912, with a bear as the quarry.

Among the commercial work Wyeth did in 1915 was one painting quite different in mood from any commercial illustration he had done before or was to do in the future. This marching group of happy children was made for the W. K. Kellogg Company of Battle Creek, Michigan. The whereabouts of the original painting is unknown, but thanks to the medium of advertising, copies of the original advertisement still exist. Other commercial assignments of those early years included paintings for Fisk Tire, Pierce-Arrow, and Blue Buckle OverAlls (Jobbers OverAll Company, Inc.).

[ 143 ]

ALASKA
Oil on canvas
Signed lower right: N. C. Wyeth
Advertisement for Cream of Wheat
Courtesy of the National Biscuit Company

Though Wyeth had written Chapin in his November 1919 letter that he had turned down all advertising work except an assignment for Winchester Arms, he must earlier that year have completed the first of his paintings for Aunt Jemima Mills, for it appeared in national magazines that autumn. By the end of World War I, the jolly-faced Aunt Jemima known and loved by a generation of Americans had begun to lose her appeal and seemed in need of rejuvenation as an advertising symbol. James Webb Young, manager of the J. Walter Thompson Company in Chicago, planned an extensive advertising campaign using a new approach—a series of ads on the theme "The Legend of Aunt Jemima," each of which would contain a choice bit of Aunt Jemima lore in the form of

THE BEAR HUNTERS
Illustration made for 1912
Winchester Arms calendar

THE BRONCO BUSTER
Oil on canvas, h:41½, w:28⅛
Signed lower right: N. C. Wyeth '06
Advertisement for Cream of Wheat
Courtesy of The Minneapolis Institute of Arts,
  Gift of The National Biscuit Company

In 1919, Wyeth made a series of illustrations
for Blue Buckle OverAlls, of which this is a representative
example.

AT THE WORLD'S FAIR IN '93
Aunt Jemima advertisement illustrated by N. C. Wyeth
Courtesy of the Quaker Oats Company

WHERE THE MAIL GOES CREAM OF WHEAT GOES
Oil on canvas, h:44¼, w:37⅞
Signed lower right: N. C. Wyeth '06
Advertisement for Cream of Wheat
Courtesy of The Minneapolis Institute of Arts,
  Gift of The National Biscuit Company

WAGNER AND LISZT
Courtesy of Steinway & Sons

an interesting narrative illustrated by a handsome, specially commissioned picture. This departure from the then standard type of advertisement had a long-lasting influence on the development of creative techniques in American advertising. During the next four or five years, N. C. Wyeth made six illustrations for the Aunt Jemima campaign, which proved to be a great success.

The year 1921 saw the appearance of four delightful paintings Wyeth made for posters. They represented the four major bank holidays —New Year's Day, the Fourth of July, Thanksgiving, and Christmas—and bore slogans designed to encourage industry and thrift.

Another group of four commercial paintings made around this time can truly be classified as fine art. They were commissioned by Steinway & Sons, for use in advertising their fine piano, "The Instrument of the Immortals." The first of the group, a masterly portrayal of the two musical giants Wagner and Liszt, was reproduced in periodicals in 1919. This was followed in 1921 by a striking composition depicting Beethoven. The third and fourth paintings were based on operas: *The King's Henchman* from Deems Taylor's opera of that name and an allegorical scene from Wagner's *Die Walküre—The Magic Fire Spell*. All four are now part of a distinguished collection of musical memorabilia

THE VIKING SHIP

THE SHIPS OF COLUMBUS

THE GOLDEN GALLEON

THE CONQUEROR

SHIP CALENDAR ILLUSTRATIONS
These four illustrations were painted for the 1923 calendar
of the Berwind-White Coal Mining Company.
Courtesy of the Delaware Art Museum

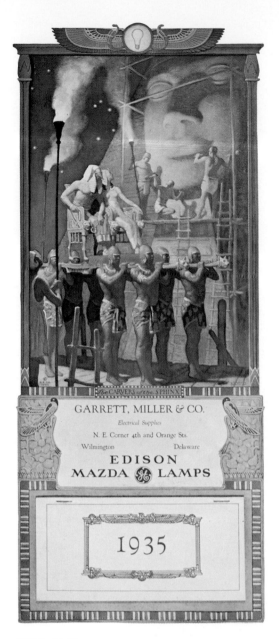

THE CARVERS OF THE SPHINX
Nela Park Division of General Electric Company 1935
    calendar
Courtesy of General Electric Company and the
    Delaware Art Museum

THE TORCH RACE
Nela Park Division of General Electric Company
    1936  calendar
Courtesy of General Electric Company and the
    Delaware Art Museum

on exhibit at Steinway Hall on West Fifty-seventh Street in New York City.

Among the many calendar illustrations Wyeth made over the years, perhaps the most beautiful and one of the most eye-appealing series is the one he made for the Berwind-White Coal Mining Company's 1923 calendar. This series consisted of four paintings of picturesque sailing ships famous for the part they played in maritime history, plus a cover illustration. It also provides an especially fine example of his talent for the effective use of scroll designs and decorative motifs.

Sometimes Wyeth's commercial work was planned to serve a dual purpose—to appear not only in magazine advertisements but also on posters. A prime example is two large paintings he made for the Interwoven Stocking Company that appeared both in the firm's advertisements and as posters in men's haberdashery stores. These two paintings received special recognition by being reproduced in the *Annual of Advertising Art: Christmas in Old Virginia* in the Seventh Annual (1928) and *The Christmas Ship in Old New York* in the Eighth Annual (1929).

In the field of commercial illustration, one of Wyeth's first commissions in the 1930s was for the Pennsylvania Railroad (now the Penn Central Transportation Company). On May 1,

BEETHOVEN AND NATURE
Courtesy of Steinway & Sons

1930, a notice was displayed in all the railroad's stations and ticket offices advising the public that

Historical posters in full color, dealing with patriotic subjects, have been designed by a well-known painter. The purpose of the new posters is not only to interest the public in the historical significance of the scenes and events portrayed, but also to emphasize the identity of the Pennsylvania Railroad with the country's growth, and its own development as a national institution.

The notice went on to say that these patriotic posters would be twelve in number, and that each would depict an outstanding scene or event in the early history and the development of the United States. However, only four of the planned twelve posters appeared, and apparently the project was dropped.

On May 22, 1930, the first poster—*Ringing Out Liberty*—was announced. It was followed on July 30 of the same year by the second one, *In Old Kentucky*. The third, *Pittsburgh in the Beginning—Fort Prince George*, was made available on November 23. The last of the announcements appeared in an undated bulletin: *"The Building of the First White House*—one of the Pennsylvania Railroad's contributions to the Washington bicentennial year." (This painting, *Building the First White Honse*, appeared on the 1971 Christmas card sent by President and Mrs. Nixon.)

[ 148 ]

PUBLIC TEST OF THE WORLD'S FIRST REAPER
Courtesy of International Harvester Company of America,
Inc.

THE CHRISTMAS SHIP IN OLD NEW YORK
Courtesy of Interwoven, Division of Kayser-Roth
Corporation

RINGING OUT LIBERTY

IN OLD KENTUCKY

PENNSYLVANIA RAILROAD PATRIOTIC POSTE
Courtesy of the Pennsylvania Railroad

PITTSBURGH IN THE BEGINNING—FORT PRINCE
GEORGE

BUILDING THE FIRST WHITE HOUSE

CUSTER'S LAST STAND
American Tobacco Company advertisement

THE FIRST KENTUCKY DERBY
Courtesy of Joseph E. Seagram & Sons, Inc.

Advertisements appearing in 1931 carried a quite different Wyeth historical picture: the first public test of the McCormick reaper at Steele's Tavern in Virginia in July of 1831. This was commissioned by the International Harvester Company to illustrate an advertisement commemorating the hundredth anniversary of the event, which had signaled the beginning of the emancipation of the American farmer. The original of this painting was destroyed in a fire.

In 1932 the American Tobacco Company launched an advertising campaign for Lucky Strike cigarettes using the slogan "Nature in the Raw is seldom Mild." The campaign included radio plugs as well as pictorial advertisements in newspapers and magazines. The paintings Wyeth made for the campaign, which really depicted "Nature in the Raw" and were definitely not "Mild," represented actual historical episodes: *The Fort Dearborn Massacre, Custer's Last Stand, The Dark and Bloody Ground, The Sea Wolf,* and *The War Whoop.*

In searching for material on N. C. Wyeth's commercial art, word-of-mouth information came to us that he had done calendar work for

General Electric Company. Then two calendars turned up in a private collection, indicating that the work had been done for General Electric's Lamp Division at Nela Park, Cleveland, Ohio.

There is an interesting bit of background information on one of these paintings. In a letter Wyeth wrote his father on September 17, 1926, he referred to having completed a calendar picture entitled *The Carvers of the Sphinx* for the Edison Mazda Company. The details he gave about it in this letter constitute an exact description of the General Electric Lamp Division calendar that came out nine years later, in 1935. *The Torch Race,* which appeared on General Electric's Lamp Division calendar in 1936, may also have been done years earlier, but there is no available documentation to support this possibility.

In the mid-thirties, Frankfort Distilleries commissioned Wyeth to paint several advertising pieces featuring their Paul Jones whiskey. The themes were related to things near and dear to Southern gentlemen and in particular to that area known as Kentucky—namely, horses and bourbon. The following titles are represen-

SAM HOUSTON
Oil on canvas, h:32, w:28
Signed lower right: N. C. Wyeth
John Morrell & Company
    calendar—"America in the
    Making," November 1940
Courtesy of Iowa State
    University, Gift of John
    Morrell & Company

tative samples: *The First Kentucky Derby; Now Major, for the best part of the game; I would like to have known my grandfather better;* and *Toby, fetch me the key to the springhouse.*

During those same years and later, Wyeth painted a number of illustrations to advertise a less potent potable, Coca-Cola. He executed no fewer than nine commissions for this company, including magazine pieces, two calendars, and several posters, among them a series of posters on the lumber and transportation industries.

During his last years, N. C. Wyeth accepted numerous calendar assignments. Those done for Hercules Incorporated and for John Morrell and Company were particularly notable; he also executed fine calendar paintings for New York Life Insurance and Brown & Bigelow, among others. His first Hercules Incorporated calendar painting, which was called *The Three Hunters,*

appeared in 1933. Those made subsequently appeared as calendars, prints, and covers for the company publication *The Hercules Mixer*, each being completed in the year immediately prior to its use. Hence, the last one, which appeared on the 1946 calendar, may well have been one of his final works of commercial art, though the painting itself bears no date. In addition to the 1933 calendar, the other Hercules Incorporated calendars were:

1934—*The Seeker*
1935—*New Trails*
1938—*The Alchemist*
1939—*A New World*
1940—*The Pioneers*
1942—*Primal Chemistry*
1944—*Sweet Land of Liberty*
1946—*The Spirit of '46*

LUMBER
One of the series of industrial posters
made for Coca-Cola in 1943
Courtesy of Coca-Cola Company

THE CONFEDERATE BATTLE FLAG—
FAITHFUL TROOPS CHEER
GENERAL LEE
Oil on panel, h:32, w:28
Signed lower right: N. C. Wyeth
John Morrell & Company calendar—"Flags in
American History," November 1944
Courtesy of the United States Naval
Academy, Annapolis, Gift of
John Morrell & Company

THE ALCHEMIST
Hercules Incorporated 1938 calendar
Courtesy of Hercules Incorporated

[ 155 ]

Wyeth's first commission for John Morrell & Company of Ottumwa, Iowa, a meat-packing company, was to do one of the twelve illustrations to be used on their 1939 calendar, which was titled "Twelve Artists Depict America." This calendar was so much in demand, particularly by schools, that the company decided to follow a historical theme—"America in the Making"—for their calendar the following year, and they asked N. C. Wyeth to make the illustrations. Again in 1941, their calendar was a Wyeth exclusive—this time on the theme "The Romance of Commerce." For their 1944 calendar they turned to him once more, to illustrate "Flags in American History."

It is known that Wyeth, in the early 1940s, made a painting of Abraham Lincoln writing the famous Bixby letter (November 21, 1864), to express sympathy to the widow who had lost her five sons on the battlefields of the Civil War. Under the title *A Cherished Memory*, the painting was commissioned by the Shaw-Barton advertising agency to be used on a calendar. Subsequently, it was used as the cover illustration for the February 1944 issue of *American Legion Magazine*, but the present owner of the painting is unknown.

The records of Brown & Bigelow reveal that Wyeth executed five paintings for them that were reproduced on calendars between 1943 and 1945. The themes were chosen to emphasize the importance of the home front during World War II, as is evidenced by the following titles: *Soldiers of the Soil, The American Flag, The Returning Soldier, The Cornhusker,* and *Lift Up Your Hearts.*

The reproductions of Wyeth's commercial work presented here, though only a varied cross-section, can certainly be considered examples of some of the finest work he did in this field. His standing as a commercial artist is further attested to by the stature of the firms who commissioned his services, many the most renowned in the saga of American enterprise.

10

# *Murals,*
# *Lunettes,*
# *and the*
# *Triptych*

Wyeth at work on *The Galleons* mural for the First National Bank of Boston. Courtesy of Mrs. N. C. Wyeth

NEWELL CONVERS WYETH was an exceptionally energetic man—he worked hard and he played hard. But play to him was felling trees, plowing a field, or running a footrace with his younger neighbors. A good deal of this virility spilled over onto his canvases. They were consistently big—as large as he could make them within the limitations of the requirements for magazine and book reproduction.

It is not surprising, therefore, that he eventually attempted that vastly larger scale of work, the mural. This kind of painting is pretty much a field in itself, and few artists who attain fame in other types of painting can—or desire to—undertake huge panoramas. Wyeth, however, gladly accepted the challenges of mural painting and executed many outstanding murals in the course of his career.

In all probability, Wyeth's first mural painting resulted from studies he submitted to the directors of the Hotel Utica Corporation as a speculative presentation, in the hope of being commissioned to do four large decorations for the grillroom of the hotel. The basic themes for

the decorations were almost identical in content to the four paintings Wyeth did to accompany "The Moods," which appeared in the December 1909 issue of *Scribner's Magazine.*

Wyeth's preliminary studies were accepted, and the murals were completed in the latter part of 1911. The Hotel Utica (Utica, New York) opened in March 1912: the murals were installed shortly before that date.

At the beginning of the Prohibition era, the Hotel Utica murals were removed from their settings and placed in storage. After Repeal, when they were taken from storage to be remounted in their original settings, it was discovered that they had deteriorated to such an extent that they could not be restored. Probably the only extant pictures of them are reproductions in color in a rare little folder put out originally as a keepsake by the Hotel Utica on the occasion of its opening. The two murals shown here—*The Indian Fisherman* and *The Indian Hunter*—are reproduced from that folder. They duplicate in theme *Summer* and *Autumn* from "The Moods" series in *Scribner's.*

## THE BATTLE OF WILSON'S CREEK

The Union forces, under Nathaniel Lyon, attempted a surprise attack on the Confederate forces commanded by General Ben McCulloch, which were encamped at Wilson's Creek, twelve miles from Springfield, Missouri. General Sterling Price is given much of the credit for the Confederate victory in this battle on August 8, 1861, one of the bloodiest in the war. Bloody Hill in the central background was the site of Totten's battery, which fired the opening guns.

Oil on canvas, h:6′, w:12′. Signed lower left: N. C. Wyeth 1920
Courtesy of the State of Missouri and the Missouri State Museum

## THE BATTLE OF WESTPORT

On the morning of October 23, 1864, Colonel John F. Phillips led a spectacular cavalry charge against General Sterling Price's Confederate cavalry, which was making a desperate rush on the Union batteries. The masses of horsemen crashed at full speed with a din that could be heard above the gunfire. This battle secured Missouri for the Union.

Oil on canvas, h:6′, w:12′. Signed lower right: N. C. Wyeth 1920
Courtesy of the State of Missouri and the Missouri State Museum

An almost exact duplicate of one of the hotel murals is Wyeth's painting *The Return of the Hunter*, which was reproduced in color in the center of fine tableware made for the hotel by the Syracuse China Corporation, of Syracuse, New York. These plates, made in various sizes, were bordered with an overglaze gold band with a maroon color line. The Wyeth painting in the center was applied by decal. On the back of each plate a special backstamp indicated that it was made expressly for the Hotel Utica. The original order for the plates was entered on August 14, 1911. Replacement orders were made in August 1937 and April 1939, but there is no record of the quantities manufactured.

Following the installation of his murals in the Hotel Utica in 1912, Wyeth was approached to do an assignment for the Washington Irving High School in New York City, which did not materialize. However, in 1915 four panoramic murals by Wyeth were mounted on the walls of the Submarine Grille of the Traymore Hotel in Atlantic City, New Jersey. In early June of that year while the murals were being completed and installed, such crowds of people came to watch that the hotel owner was compelled to put a notice in the newspaper announcing that the room would be closed to the public until the pictures were completely finished and in place. After World War II the Grille was redecorated and the murals were removed. It is not known what disposition was made of them. The rare photographs from which the reproductions in this chapter were made were generously supplied by Mrs. Andrew Wyeth.

In January of 1920 interest was shown in having N. C. Wyeth paint several lunettes for the Missouri state capitol in Jefferson City. The building was new, completed only in 1918 on a bluff overlooking the Missouri River and the rich farmlands beyond. The State Capitol Decorating Committee had decided to have the corridors decorated with lunette murals six feet high by twelve feet wide depicting incidents in the history of the state, and commissioned Wyeth to do two of them. The lunettes were unveiled on January 9, 1921.

In April of 1920 there was some discussion about Wyeth's painting murals for the Buccaneer Room of the new Flamingo Hotel in Miami, but the idea apparently came to naught. However, by August he had accepted a commission to paint two murals for the Federal

THE RETURN OF THE HUNTER
Reproduced on tableware made by the Syracuse China Corporation for the Hotel Utica. The plate shown is ten inches in diameter.
Courtesy of Onondaga Pottery Company (Syracuse China Corporation).

Reserve Bank of Boston. These, each approximately twelve feet high by ten feet wide, still decorate opposite walls of the junior officers' quarters at the bank.

Even though Wyeth remained deeply involved with book illustration, more and more mural commissions came his way. A letter to his friend Joseph Chapin of Scribner's is indicative of his feelings about the work:

> Personally speaking, an outstanding event for me will be the arrangements already made to devote about ⅓ of my time to study under George Noyes (an obscure painter but a marvelous colorist). I need this help beyond words! Mural work is looming up importantly and I must know more definitely the science of color:—this knowledge added to certain instinctive feelings I have regarding it should mean much.[1]

Throughout the 1920s Wyeth turned out mural masterpieces with regularity. Although a planned assignment for the Highland Park High School in Highland Park, Illinois, was canceled, he did at least thirteen murals and panels for

THE HUNTER
Oil on canvas
Hotel Utica Mural
Courtesy of Mrs. Andrew Wyeth

THE FISHERMAN
Oil on canvas
Hotel Utica Mural
Courtesy of Mrs. Andrew Wyeth

IN THE DARK DAYS OF THE CIVIL WAR
Oil on canvas, h:12′, w:10′
Signed lower right: N. C. Wyeth 1922
The mural depicts Lincoln and Secretary of
    the Treasury Salmon P. Chase.
Courtesy of the Federal Reserve Bank of Boston

five edifices during the balance of the decade. One of these was *The Giant,* a memorial decoration made for the Westtown School of Westtown, Pennsylvania, in 1923. This large canvas, six feet high by five feet wide, embellishes the dining room of the long-established school. *The Giant* was painted as a memorial to a very popular student who had died at an early age—William Clothier Engle, a boy with high ideals, a fine sense of humor, and a distinct talent for art. When this young friend and student of N. C. Wyeth's died, Wyeth consented to do the mural and took great pains to choose a theme he felt the lad would have appreciated. The locale of the painting was Beach Haven, New Jersey, where both Engle and the Wyeth children had enjoyed summer holidays. The Wyeth children appear in the painting.

By the spring of 1924 he had completed five other murals—for the First National Bank of Boston: four ship murals and a map mural that surrounded a large impressive doorway. Of this commission Wyeth wrote:

When I was first commissioned to do the work, the portraying of incidents associated with Boston history was considered. But this seemed too local and confining. Ships and the sea had been much in my dreams for years. Visions of canvasses, alive with moving water, sailing clouds and flying ships, seemed at last within my grasp. In pondering as to what would relate to the bank's commercial activities and retain the infinite spirit of the sea, I evolved the idea of cargo carriers.

Four historic periods of shipping finally were chosen, represented by Phoenician biremes, Elizabethan galleons, clipper ships and tramp steamers.[2]

That same year (1924) saw the installation of his great mural in the Hotel Roosevelt in New York City. This consisted of three panels, the center one of which depicted the sturdy little Dutch ship *Half Moon* gliding up the Hudson before a fair autumn wind that whipped the river into serried whitecaps, with the soaring Palisades as a background. Wyeth selected this 1609 event as his theme not only for its historic aptness but as a tribute to the Dutch, for the Netherlands was the ancestral home of the world-famed American statesman and native New Yorker for whom the hotel is named. From the deck of the *Half Moon,* sailors are watching the looming highlands in wonder while, in the

AN APOTHEOSIS OF FRANKLIN
Oil on canvas, h:30', w:16'
Signed lower right: N. C. Wyeth
Courtesy of the Franklin Savings Bank, New York City

side panels, Indians gaze at the winged intruder from behind a tracery of birches, alders, and cottonwood saplings.

The year 1925 was marked by the completion of a huge mural—*An Apotheosis of Franklin*—decorating the east wall on the main floor of

Hotel Traymore Mural
Oil on canvas, h:8′, w:20′
Courtesy of Mrs. Andrew Wyeth

the Franklin Savings Bank at Forty-second Street and Eighth Avenue in New York City. This was approximately thirty feet high by sixteen feet wide.

For the second floor of the National Geographic Society headquarters in Washington, Wyeth did a series of five murals, which were completed in 1927. At that time, the magazine offices were largely concentrated in the Gardner Greene Hubbard Memorial, a building dedicated in the early part of the century as a tribute to the founder of that world-renowned publication. Today, the magazine headquarters is a new steel and glass building on Seventeenth Street, behind its former location, and the Gardner Greene Hubbard Memorial is little used in comparison to former years and is virtually closed to the public. But the murals remain in place on the upper level, reached by a circular stairway. Consideration was once given to transferring them to the new building, but no suitable area was available to display them. Full-color sup-

plements reproducing the murals were published as part of the March, May, July, and November 1928 issues and the January 1929 issue of the *National Geographic Magazine.*

Toward the end of the 1920s, Wyeth wrote to Chapin at Scribner's:

Regarding Gulliver. I am selected by the Massachusetts Art Commission to execute six panels for the State House in Boston. At present, the problem is to get the Ways and Means Committee to appropriate the funds. This is a memorial to the First General Court Meeting in Massachusetts which took place in 1630; so if it goes through O.K. these panels must be done as soon as possible. Before giving you a decision on Gulliver I must await the outcome of the State House matter. I ought to hear most any day.[3]

Apparently the funds were never appropriated—at any rate, Wyeth never carried out any such assignment in the State House in Boston. However, during the 1930s he completed six more magnificent wall decorations, the first doubtless being the mural for the First Mechanics National Bank of Trenton, New Jersey (now the First Trenton National Bank). The subject was General Washington's entrance into Trenton on his way to New York to be inaugurated as our first President.

Records show that the general and his suite arrived on the opposite bank of the river at Colvin's Ferryhouse at two o'clock on the afternoon of April 21, 1789, and Patrick Colvin ferried them across the Delaware. At Trenton Landing, near the tavern of Rensselaer Williams, the party was met by leading citizens of Trenton with appropriate ceremonies, and then the assemblage escorted the travelers into the village proper. There the general and his suite mounted the horses that had been readied for them, and proceeded up the Ferry Road and thence toward the bridge over Assunpink Creek, where the matrons and young ladies of the village had superintended the erection of a beautiful arch.

Wyeth was always a stickler for historic accuracy in his paintings and researched his themes and scenes very thoroughly. A careful examination of the details in this Trenton bank mural seems to indicate he may have been influenced by a contemporary account of the arch and the details of Washington's entrance into Trenton that was published in *Columbian Magazine*, May 1789.

While Wyeth was overseeing the installation of the Trenton bank mural from a scaffold high above the marble floor, it is said that he slipped and almost fell. The frightening experience haunted him and resulted in a dream, the essence of which he put on canvas: *In a Dream I Meet General Washington*. This was awarded the fourth William A. Clarke Prize in the 1932 Corcoran Biennial.

During the years 1930 and 1931 Wyeth also worked hard on another mural—*The Apotheosis of the Family*—to have it ready in time to dedicate at the centennial of the Wilmington Savings Fund, which was founded in 1832. This, one of the largest single murals in the United States (nineteen feet high by sixty feet long), was painted on heavy canvas and mounted in five

[ 163 ]

THE PHOENICIAN BIREMES
Oil on canvas, h:15′, w:12′
Signed lower right: N. C. Wyeth 1923
Courtesy of the First National Bank of Boston

THE TRAMP STEAMER
Oil on canvas, h:15′, w:12′
Signed lower left: N. C. Wyeth
Courtesy of the First National Bank of Boston

THE DISCOVERER
Published March 1928
Oil on canvas, h:7'10⅜", w:30'2"
Signed lower right: N. C. Wyeth 1927
© 1928 National Geographic Society

sections spanning the entire south wall of the Wilmington Savings Fund Society building.

At first, the officers of the society had been in a quandary as to what type of decoration might be given the long blank wall. Frederic E. Stone, then the president, thought the best solution would be a large mural on a theme compatible with the business of the organization—the story of thrift as it applies to humanity—and he consulted with N. C. Wyeth, who happened to be a close personal friend. For a full year Wyeth mulled over ideas for projecting the concept of family solidarity and integrity as the basic structure upon which civilization is built. He concluded that only an allegorical painting with a theme focused on the family would be appropriate for the Savings Fund's hundredth anniversary.

After making preliminary sketches, Wyeth did a finely executed oil study to scale, and it was from this that the mural was painted. In all, it took him a year and a half to complete his grand conception. Dominating the center of the picture is the group symbolizing Home and the Family. From left to the center, and from the center to right, the seasons merge from spring to summer and from fall to winter, and so the observer's eye moves from one kind of human activity to another, ever aware of man's varied labors and of the influence of nature's fundamental forces. In its overall effect, the mural is like a symphonic presentation.[4]

Wyeth wrote a very detailed explanation of the mural he painted for the main lobby of the Penn Mutual Life Insurance Company office in Philadelphia, *William Penn, Man of Courage–Vision–Action*. This painting, completed in the fall of 1932 and mounted on the first of February the following year, is fourteen feet high by ten and a half feet wide.

Wyeth's next mural was commissioned to celebrate an anniversary—the first half century of the Silver Burdett Company's service to education. Titled *The Spirit of Education*, this painting was originally housed in the company's New York office, but when their new headquarters in Morristown, New Jersey, were completed in 1955, it was moved there, where it dominates the main entrance foyer.

By the spring of 1936, Wyeth had completed a truly magnificent mural—the triptych in the Chapel of the Holy Spirit at the Washington Cathedral (Episcopal), which is one of the great cathedrals of the world, exceeded in area by only five others. As visitors wander through this vast edifice, properly called the Cathedral

Church of Saint Peter and Saint Paul, they eventually come to the Chapel of the Holy Spirit, and after passing through iron gates and grilles lacelike in design they are confronted by beautiful oak-paneled reredos and Wyeth's triptych.

No one could better describe this great work of Wyeth's than John H. Bayless, curator at the cathedral for almost forty years. He has lived with the triptych since its inception:

> I watched every stroke of his brush. The mural was painted on Gesso which Mr. Wyeth built layer by layer with painstaking effort.
>
> The seven gifts of the Holy Spirit are symbolized by the doves at the base of the triptych. In the center panel, the figure of Christ seems almost to be moving forward suggesting the 28th verse of the eleventh chapter of the Gospel According to Saint Matthew, "Come Unto Me, All Ye That Labor and are Heavy Laden, and I Will Give You Rest". The feeling of motion is produced by the rays of glory about the Figure (strips of gilded wood glued to the wood and planed from the extremities to the point where they meet the figure flush with the surface of the painting). "I Am the True Vine and Ye are the Branches Thereof" is suggested by the motif above

the figure. The two side panels portray angels in motion, symbolic of the Holy Spirit.

In the dining room of St. Andrew's School, Middletown, Delaware, is a Wyeth mural commissioned by Mrs. Irénée duPont, who, with her brother, A. Felix duPont, donated the original funds for the school.[5] The June 6, 1936, issue of the school paper, *The Cardinal*, announced, "The mural now being executed by N. C. Wyeth will cover the east wall of the dining room." Progress was reported six months later in the January issue—the mural was "now well under way, and is expected to be finished by the dedication services, April 14th."

The headmaster's report in June of that year had this to say of it:

> Mrs. Irénée duPont's fine gift of a mural for the Dining Room has been more than half finished by the painter, Mr. N. C. Wyeth, and to all who have seen it, seems a thrilling symbol of the School's conception and realization.

Over a year later came this report:

On September 1st [1938] Mr. N. C. Wyeth placed on the Dining Room wall the long

HALF MOON IN THE HUDSON (left panel)

HALF MOON IN THE HUDSON (center panel)

HALF MOON IN THE HUDSON TRIPTYCH
Oil on canvas, each panel, h:14', w:8'
Right panel signed lower right: N. C. Wyeth 1924
Courtesy of the Hotel Roosevelt

HALF MOON IN THE HUDSON (right panel)

GENERAL WASHINGTON'S ENTRANCE INTO
TRENTON
Oil on canvas, h:17½', w:12'
Signed lower left: N. C. Wyeth 1930; lower right: ©
First Mechanics National Bank of Trenton
Courtesy of First Trenton National Bank
Photograph courtesy of the Edward Seal Collection

THE APOTHEOSIS OF THE FAMILY
Oil on canvas, h:19', w:60'
Signed bottom center: N. C. Wyeth 1931
Courtesy of Wilmington Savings Fund Society

MAP OF DISCOVERY—EASTERN HEMISPHERE
Published November 1928
Oil on canvas: h:7′11⅛″, w:9′3⅜″
Signed lower left: N. C. Wyeth 1927
© 1928 National Geographic Society


MAP OF DISCOVERY—WESTERN HEMISPHERE
Published January 1929
Oil on canvas, h:7′11½″, w:8′11⅞″
Signed lower right: N. C. Wyeth 1927
© 1929 National Geographic Society

Right-hand part of St. Andrew's School mural
Oil on canvas
Courtesy of St. Andrew's School and the Reverend
    Robert A. Moss, Headmaster

THE COMING OF THE MAYFLOWER
Oil on canvas, h:9', w:13¼'
Signed lower left: N. C. Wyeth
Courtesy of the Metropolitan Life Insurance Company

expected mural. This remarkable painting has exceeded even the highest expectations for it, and will be a focal point of inspiration for many generations of St. Andreans.

The left portion of the mural shows Alma Mater seated on her throne amidst the boys of St. Andrew's. It is said that at first Wyeth strove for realistic likenesses of specific students, but it was decided that anonymity was preferable. So the boys were finally painted from the artist's imagination.

The right-hand side of the mural pictures the charter trustees of the Episcopal Church School Foundation, Inc., through which Mr. duPont founded and endowed the school, and several notables who, though not of this group, were greatly engrossed in the activities. The group is depicted examining and discussing the blueprints for the school. The English cathedrals —Canterbury and St. Paul's—which appear in the misty background, represent the Anglican Church tradition on which the school's life and worship were based. The portraits of the men in the group are true likenesses. Each of them posed for Wyeth, and he also attended meetings of the trustees so that he could observe the typical role and attitude of each man.

The last mural commission Wyeth accepted was one he looked forward to doing with a very special sense of happiness and enthusiasm. The assignment was actually a series of murals on the grand scale, to serve as a graphic and dramatic expression of the spirit of New England: *The Coming of the Mayflower* and *The Departure of the Mayflower*, along with six others— *First Harvest*, *The Turkey Hunt*, *The Thanksgiving Feast*, *Going to Church*, *Priscilla and John Alden*, and *The Wedding Procession*.

Throughout his lifetime Wyeth never lost sight of or failed to convey to others his pride in his New England heritage.

New England was where I was born, raised and educated. I felt, therefore, that of all the subjects possible, this was the one I knew best. The romance of early colonization, especially that of the Pilgrims in Massachusetts, had always excited me. My ancestor, Nicholas Wyeth, came from Wales to Massachusetts in 1647. The spirit of early days on the Massachusetts coast was an oft-discussed subject in my home.

I was born in Needham, not far from the town of Plymouth, to which I made many pilgrimages during my boyhood, spending thrilling days in and around that historic territory. With this as a background,

THE TURKEY HUNT
Oil on canvas, section shown, h:7′, w:28¾′; section
    not shown, h:7′, w:13½′
Unsigned
Courtesy of the Metropolitan Life Insurance Company

THE THANKSGIVING FEAST
Oil on canvas, section shown, h:7′, w:23′; section not
    shown, h:7′, w:23⅔′
Signed lower left: N. C. Wyeth
Courtesy of the Metropolitan Life Insurance Company

THE WEDDING PROCESSION
Oil on canvas, h:7′, w:25¼′
Unsigned
Courtesy of the Metropolitan Life Insurance Company

HERONS IN SUMMER
Oil on canvas, h:6¾', w:13'
Unsigned
Courtesy of the Metropolitan Life Insurance Company

MALLARD DUCKS IN SPRING
Oil on canvas, h:10½', w:13'
Signed lower right: N. C. Wyeth
Courtesy of the Metropolitan Life Insurance Company

it was natural that my mind and heart should fly to Plymouth and to the Pilgrims as a fitting and appropriate subject for a series of New England paintings.

If then, the warmth and appeal of these paintings is apparent to those who study them, it is principally because they are, in some related way, a statement of my own life and heritage. All creative expression, be it in painting, writing, or music, if it pretends to appeal warmly and eloquently, must spring from the artist's own factual and emotional experience.[6]

Thus began the planning of his final work in the field of mural painting in the latter part of 1939. He was to devote much of the next six years to it, though he was not destined to see its completion. On an October morning in 1945 tragedy struck—the artist's hand was stilled forever in a railroad-crossing accident. What more fitting memorial could there have been than that Wyeth's younger son, Andrew, now America's most popular living artist, and his son-in-law John McCoy should complete the work he had begun?

[ 171 ]

TRIPTYCH—Chapel of the Holy Spirit
Oil on canvas
Courtesy of Eston Photo Reproductions, New York

The great panorama of the Pilgrim murals is not all the Wyeth bounty housed in the main office of the Metropolitan Life Insurance Company in New York City. There are also four handsome panels depicting aquatic and game birds.

From time to time, various articles have appeared that made reference to N. C. Wyeth's having painted other murals besides those shown and discussed here. After carefully investigating these reports, we are convinced that the paintings reproduced in this chapter represent his total output of murals—certainly a bountiful heritage from one who was at the same time steadily fulfilling book, magazine, and advertising commissions and creating numerous easel paintings that rank with the best done by his peers.

SEPTEMBER AFTERNOON (1918)
Oil on canvas, h:42, w:48
Signed lower right: N. C. Wyeth
Courtesy of Mrs. N. C. Wyeth

# 11 *Easel Painting*

THE name N. C. Wyeth is, by most people, instantly and invariably associated with the fine illustrations he made for books and magazines, in particular those he painted for the classics that were published by Charles Scribner's Sons, Cosmopolitan Book Corporation, and David Mc-Kay. Without doubt he is best remembered for these because they impressed young readers both consciously and subconsciously, and thereby remained with them as an integral part of the growing-up experience.

However, from his earliest days as an illustrator, Wyeth had expressed a desire to become a landscape painter, and had had many conversations about this with his teacher Howard Pyle, who encouraged him to devote part of his time

[ 173 ]

Peter Minuet

PETER MINUIT
Oil on canvas, h:42, w:30
Signed lower right: N. C. Wyeth 1926
(This portrait hung in New York's Hotel Roosevelt
and is believed to have been painted to complement
the mural *Half Moon on the Hudson.*)
Courtesy of Edward Eberstadt & Sons, New York

to such paintings. With his deep love of nature and the out-of-doors, it is easy to understand why Wyeth would find particular satisfaction in expressing these feelings in landscapes and seascapes depicting either his beloved Brandywine country or the environs of his summer home at Port Clyde, Maine.

Wyeth attributed much of his success in the field of both illustration and easel painting to an early teacher, Charles W. Reed, who taught him that observation must be converted to memory, for without training this faculty, mood and imagination would be lacking in the artist's work. Wyeth took this advice to heart, and later in life he said:

Every illustration or painting I have made has been done from the imagination or the

memory. However, I have constantly studied from the figure, from animals and from landscape, and have especially stressed the training of my memory.[1]

His many years of self-discipline in converting observation to memory resulted in his beautiful painting *Summer Night*, completed in 1942, to name one example. Wyeth recalled the circumstances:

One summer's night several years ago, during one of my familiar walks along the broad stretches of the Brandywine Meadows, I passed among a herd of dairy cows quietly standing and lying down in the bright moonlight. It was sultry, and great threatening clouds moved and lifted in

[ 174 ]

ANN STUYVESANT
Oil on canvas, h:42, w:30
Signed lower left: N. C. Wyeth 1926
(Like the portrait of Peter Minuit, this too is
believed to have been made to complement the
mural *Half Moon on the Hudson*.)
Courtesy of Edward Eberstadt & Sons, New York

STILL LIFE WITH APPLES (1918)
Oil on canvas, h:32⅛, w:40⅛
Unsigned

[ 175 ]

A MAINE SEA CAPTAIN'S DAUGHTER
Tempera on panel, h:29½, w:22¾
Signed upper left: N. C. Wyeth
Courtesy of William R. Rollins

STILL LIFE WITH BRUSH
Oil on canvas, h:16, w:20
Signed lower right: N. C. Wyeth
Courtesy of B. F. Schlimme

FENCE BUILDERS
Oil on canvas, h:37½, w:49½
Signed lower right: N. C. Wyeth 1915
Courtesy of Carl D. Pratt

LAST OF THE CHESTNUTS (*Tree Cutters*) (1917)
Oil on canvas, h:37, w:49
Signed lower right: N. C. Wyeth
Courtesy of Diamond M Foundation, Snyder, Texas

SUMMER DAYS (circa 1910)
Oil on canvas, h:16, w:20
Unsigned
Courtesy of Mr. & Mrs. Andrew Wyeth

[ 177 ]

NEWBORN CALF (*Cows in Moonlight*)
Oil on canvas, h:42, w:47
Signed lower left: N. C. Wyeth 1917
Courtesy of Mrs. Andrew Wyeth

majestic patterns across the sky line like the silent shifting of scenery on a celestial stage.

The full moon threw shafts of clear mellow light through the cloud openings which slowly swung across the dark terrain like beams from a beatific searchlight.

As I watched the impressive spectacle before me, I became conscious that one of the cows, standing apart from the main groups of reposing animals, was in labor and about to drop her calf.

I watched the progress of this miracle of birth for a long time, in fact until the new bit of life on earth finally struggled to its feet, cast its own new shadow, and wobbled and fumbled its way to its mother's teats and drenched itself in warm milk.

Many times since then I have attempted to express the mood of this impressive experience in pattern and color.[2]

Throughout his career N. C. Wyeth was constantly referred to as an illustrator, a label he deeply resented, not because laymen used it in referring to him, but because those in the art world looked down from their ivory towers and deprecated illustration as a second-rate art form. He once wrote:

> There is a very depressing belief in artistic circles, particularly among the painters themselves, that illustration is not an art but a craft, that it is not conceived from inspirational sources, but is built and fashioned as a stage setting would be around the theme of a story, or planned like an ingenious design. The painter's opinion of the illustrator's profession as compared to his own, is often very near that of contempt.[3]

In speaking before a class conducted by another renowned former student of the Howard Pyle School, Harvey Dunn, Wyeth was somewhat startled by the general attitude of the students: they wanted to be illustrators so that they could make money and become artists.

"Fine," he commented, "but the only trouble is that you've got to be an artist before you can be an illustrator."[4]

Illustration was and still remains, to a degree, an inferior form in the eyes of certain art critics, art experts, and others who consider themselves highly knowledgeable. Many of them spurn or ignore work they term "commercial" but go into ecstasies over the efforts of others made famous only through public relations media. In actuality, few are the great artists of history who were not illustrators. Their pictures told stories of the places, the customs, and the incidents in the lives of their people. Our own Winslow Homer and John Sloan were illustrators before they were "discovered" and "saved" from that stigma.

Despite Wyeth's success in the field of book and magazine illustration and his prominence as a mural painter, he constantly strove to rise above the label he so detested. He cherished the rare moments when he was free of commitments and could retire to the countryside of his beloved Chadds Ford or the Maine seacoast to sketch and paint the things that he knew best and that stirred him most—neighbors at work in the field, a rural scene, a quaint old house, a salty lobsterman—the simple native themes of his finest paintings.

In 1915, Wyeth was hard at work on a large easel painting, *The Fence Builders*. This may have been his first truly serious effort to

BUTTONWOOD FARM (1920)
Oil on canvas, h:48½, w:42½
Signed lower right: N. C. Wyeth
Courtesy of The Reading Public Museum
and Art Gallery, Reading, Pa.

CANNIBAL SHORE (1930)
Oil on canvas, h:30, w:47
Signed lower left: N. C. Wyeth
Courtesy of William A. Farnsworth Library
and Art Museum, Rockland, Maine

SOUNDING SEA (Black Head, Monhegan Island) (1934)
Oil on canvas, h:48¼, w:52¼
Signed lower left: N. C. Wyeth
Courtesy of Mr. & Mrs. Joseph E. Levine

CORN HARVEST ON THE
    BRANDYWINE (1936)
Oil on canvas, w:52, h:48
Signed lower right: N. C. Wyeth 193-
*The Progressive Farmer* (cover), November
    1936 & October 1946
Courtesy of the North Carolina Museum
    of Art, Raleigh

STILL LIFE WITH IRIS AND ORANGES
Oil on canvas, h:36, w:40
Signed lower right: N. C. Wyeth
Courtesy of the Delaware Art Museum

SUMMER NIGHT (1942)
Tempera on panel, h:22, w:36
Signed lower left: N. C. Wyeth
Courtesy of Mr. and Mrs. Bruce Bredin

THE HUPPER FARM (*Evening*) (1939)
Tempera on panel, h:24¾, w:39¾
Signed lower right: N. C. Wyeth
Courtesy of the Dallas Museum of Fine Arts,
  Gift of C. R. Smith

ISLAND FUNERAL (1939)
Tempera on wood, h:44, w:52
Signed upper left: N. C. Wyeth
Courtesy of Hotel DuPont, Wilmington

DEEP COVE LOBSTERMAN (1939)
Oil on panel, h:19, w:25
Signed lower right: N. C. Wyeth
Courtesy of The Pennsylvania Academy of the Fine Arts

SUN GLINT (1938)
Tempera on panel, h:25, w:31
Signed lower left: N. C. Wyeth
Courtesy of The New Britain Museum of American Art,
Harriet Russell Stanley Memorial

do a canvas that would not be associated with illustration as such. He spent the better part of the spring of that year working on it, and in letters to his family one can sense his feeling of accomplishment.

The influence of one Giovanni Segantini, whom Wyeth greatly admired, was apparent in a number of his easel paintings over the next few years. The use of pure color bordered by gradations of white heightened the brilliancy of the color pigment, and his experimentation in the technique of Segantini resulted in several outstanding paintings, among which were *Newborn Calf, September Afternoon,* and *Buttonwood Farm.*

To achieve recognition as a painter became an obsession. Despite the many requests he received to illustrate stories for books and magazines and anticipated commissions for mural paintings and commercial artwork, the pressures within him demanded that he strive to reach that higher pinnacle.

I have passed through two months of the worst depression I ever remember. I have been highly conscious of certain serious artistic weaknesses that stand between me and the next step ahead. Only thorough application will overcome the difficulty I guess.[5]

In yet another letter he concerned himself with the work of a well-known author of the· time, and the parallels between writing and painting.

His enthusiasm is great! and his craft is highly appealing. But this to me does not conceal a remarkable lack of earthiness—of sound basic appeal, a primal quality which must exist in an artist's work as a foundation wall exists under a house.

One can feel the very curvature of the earth's surface in John Constable's landscapes; a seemingly lost power to even our best landscapists today. Just as in Homer, Tolstoi and Whitman we can feel the earth in its cycle in spite of the sharp movements and distractions of passing human incidents.

And this power can come but from one source—from life lived deeply—from contact felt, the results of bodily feeling and not of mental conjuring. Millet's peasants work with backs bent from a toil that he had

LOBSTERING OFF BLACK SPRUCE LEDGE (1939)
Tempera on panel, h:42, w:52
Signed lower left

experienced; the hoes and mattocks they grip in their hands have the "feel" and weight that only a man who had used them could interpret. Rembrandt's heads are profound because fundamentally he loved the very structure, weight and substance of the head from the front back through the skull. There is material as well as spiritual identification required for this standard of creative art.

My axiom of art is the old, old one that we can only produce vitally what we are bodily—no more. An artificial life begets artificiality—no more, although artificiality can be superlatively dressed up on occasion I'll admit.[6]

Through the early twenties Wyeth accepted the challenge of what would seem a staggering amount of work for most artists. Mural commis-

THE LOBSTERMAN (*Hauling in a Light Fog*)
*Trending into Maine*, by Kenneth Roberts
Little, Brown and Company, 1938

CORN HARVEST (1943)
Tempera on panel, h:31, w:34
Signed lower left: N. C. Wyeth
Courtesy of the Wilmington Trust Company

sions flooded in, but with the tremendous vitality that characterized him, he turned them out one after another—and then went back to his experimentation. Painting simple still life canvases gave him a chance to test his handling of light, depth of color, and form. A demijohn, for example, taken from a shelf after years of undisturbed slumber, provided an opportunity to interpret a concrete object—its shape, the light pattern, the dust; a vase of iris and a dish of oranges—color harmony, light, and form of a different nature.

Wyeth did not find such work "stupid or pottering." He did it for "practice and self-dis-

cipline, especially since such concrete work" helped him to

avoid the danger of generalizing too much in his painting. Combined with the discipline [was] the joy in feeling the form of objects, in observing the light and in knowing that such training [was] a sort of investment which [would] yield greater return by being stored up and augmented.[7]

The July 1925 issue of the *Ladies' Home Journal* contained an article about Wyeth and his art:

[ 184 ]

THE DORYMAN (*Evening*)
Oil on canvas, h:42, w:35
Signed lower right: N. C. Wyeth/Port Clyde/Maine
*Trending into Maine,* by Kenneth Roberts
Little, Brown and Company, 1938
Courtesy of Mrs. Norman B. Woolworth

DARK HARBOR FISHERMAN (1943)
Tempera on panel, h:35, w:38
Signed lower left: N. C. Wyeth
Courtesy of Robert F. Woolworth

MRS. CUSHMAN'S HOUSE (1942)
Tempera on panel, h:21, w:36½
Signed lower left: N. C. Wyeth
Courtesy of the New Britain Museum of American

N. C. Wyeth's ambition is to be a painter. He is today the most outstanding figure among the younger American decorators and an illustrator of real note. In the eyes of most, these achievements would stamp him as a painter of the first water, but that Wyeth is more exacting in his self-appraisal is characteristic of his modesty.

By the end of the nineteen twenties Wyeth's prodigious output of book and magazine illustration had dwindled to a trickle in comparison with former years. He became more and more involved with his serious painting.

The past year has been, I believe, a critical and important one for me, artistically. I have, at any rate, worked myself into a position from which I can see years of exciting and progressive adventure.[8]

Throughout the thirties and early forties, he spaced out his acceptance of commissions for murals, book illustrations, and considerable work in the field of commercial art so that, between assignments, he could devote some time to painting subjects of his own choice.

These paintings materialized, not in the rapid fashion that had marked his earlier work in illustration. Weeks, sometimes months, were spent on the preliminary composition and the preparation of the panel. For the most part done in tempera, these pictures were created by the slow and methodical buildup of color and glaze.

After all the many years of Wyeth's dedication to art he finally had his day—December 4, 1939, the opening of his first one-man show at

THE ROAD TO THE JONES HOUSE (1939)
Tempera on panel, h:22, w:40
Signed lower right: N. C. Wyeth
Courtesy of the Dallas Museum of Fine Arts, Gift
    of C. R. Smith

IN PENOBSCOT BAY
Tempera on panel, h:23¼, w:47½
Signed lower right: N. C. Wyeth 1942
Courtesy of Amanda K. Berls

THE SPRINGHOUSE
Tempera on wood, h:36, w:48
Signed lower left: N. C. Wyeth 1944
Courtesy of Delaware Art Museum

NIGHTFALL (1945)
Tempera on wood, h:31¾, w:40
Signed lower left: N. C. Wyeth
Courtesy of Robert F. Woolworth

the old MacBeth Galleries in New York City, which included a number of his finest paintings, most of them of recent vintage. The center of attraction was perhaps his recently completed *Island Funeral*, along with a number of others depicting the Maine scene.

Wyeth's son-in-law Peter Hurd, a fine artist in his own right, had this to say in his introduction to the show catalogue:

The paintings are the product of revolt against the inevitable limitation of the art of illustration which Mr. Wyeth has long served with sincerity and grace. Of the illustrator's heritage he takes freely and consciously those components which may relate to painting—a strongly dramatic presentation but one freed from the paraphernalia of archeology; an ability to establish vividly

[ 189 ]

PENNSYLVANIA FARMER *(Portrait of a Farmer)* (1943)
Tempera on panel, h:40, w:60
Unsigned
Courtesy of Robert F. Woolworth

Preliminary Study for *Pennsylvania Farmer*
*(Portrait of a Farmer)*
Courtesy of Mrs. N. C. Wyeth

N. C. Wyeth outside his studio, circa 1944.
Photograph by William E. Phelps
Courtesy of William Penn Memorial Museum, Harrisburg

N. C. Wyeth, 1944
Photograph by William E. Phelps
Courtesy of the Delaware Art Museum

the quality of a certain moment in which he unfolds the observer and causes him to see, to hear, and above all, to feel. He compels us to stop and ponder with him the surrounding vision of form and color, of radiance and shadow. This world of his is at once grave and lyric.

In 1941 Wyeth was recognized by those who had frowned on illustration as a second-rate art form—he was elected to the National Academy. And in June of 1945 he received a further distinction—the honorary degree of Master of Arts from Bowdoin College. In between these years, great paintings materialized: *Black Spruce Ledge, Summer Night, In Penobscot Bay, Mrs. Cushman's House, Pennsylvania Farmer, Dark Harbor Fishermen, The Spring House,* and *Nightfall.*

Since the tragic accident on that October day in 1945 that took the life of N. C. Wyeth, the years have tested his merit as an artist. His works, like the paintings of some others who were belittled as illustrators, are now diligently sought and collected by the very people who once spurned them.

N. C. Wyeth, Port Clyde, Maine
Courtesy of Mrs. N. C. Wyeth

DR. CLAPTON
Oil on canvas, h:40, w:30
Signed lower right: W
*Drums,* by James Boyd
Charles Scribner's Sons, 1928
Courtesy of J. N. Bartfield

# With Gratitude

A BOOK that must basically depend upon the assistance of others should identify those people whose generosity helped to make it possible. Such is the purpose of the section usually known as Acknowledgments, but that word does not adequately express our feeling toward the many individuals and organizations that assisted us in the completion of this work on N.C. Wyeth. We mention them here with very special gratitude:

Mrs. N.C. Wyeth and Mr. and Mrs. Andrew Wyeth, who gave generously of their own private collections, their time, and their encouragement; also Miss Carolyn Wyeth and Mrs. John McCoy II.

The late Helen L. Card, who supplied invaluable bibliographical material from her extensive files on American illustrators, and Ronald R. Randall, of John Howell—Books, a Wyeth specialist who also supplied bibliographic material.

Richard Layton, former curator of the Brandywine River Museum, whose unfailing support included aid in locating many of the owners of Wyeth paintings.

Henry Chachowski, photographer extraordinary, who devoted much of his time and talent to photographing many of the pictures contained in this book, and to Beatrice Dunn.

Mrs. Kathryn Pinney, who edited this book, and George Hornby, who designed it.

Russell Barnet Aitken
Charles Allmond III
American Airlines
  Miss Kathleen Coy
American Tobacco Company
  M. V. Timlen
John F. Apgar, Jr.
Mrs. Sidney Ashcraft
J. N. Bartfield Galleries, Inc., New York
George Beck
Leroy Benge, Sr.
Miss Amanda K. Berls
Walter Bimson
Brandywine River Museum, Chadds
  Ford, Pa.
  Andrew Johnson, Director
  Mrs. Barbara DiFilippo
  Mrs. Anne Mayer
  Miss Jennifer Taylor
Mr. and Mrs. J. Bruce Bredin
Mrs. Gertrude H. Britton
The Brooklyn Museum
  Arno Jakobson
  Susanne P. Sack
Brown & Bigelow
  M. W. Eichers
Mr. and Mrs. R. R. M. Carpenter, Jr.
*Civil War Times Illustrated*
  Frederic Ray
John Clymer
Coca-Cola Company
  Wilbur G. Kurtz, Jr.
  Marshall H. Lane
Coe Kerr Galleries, Inc., New York
Colby College Art Museum,
  Waterville, Maine
  Hugh J. Gourley III
Mrs. Russell G. Colt
Jerome Connolly
Dallas Museum of Fine Art
  Merrill C. Reuppel
Delaware Art Museum, Wilmington
  Bruce St. John, Director

Roland Elzea, Curator of Collections
  Mrs. Phyllis Nixon
  Mrs. A. Burton Stanhope
Mr. and Mrs. Richard DeVictor
Diamond M Foundation, Snyder, Texas
  Mrs. Waunita Strayhorn
Hon. James S. Douglas
Downe Publishing, Inc.,
  and *The Ladies' Home Journal*
Edward Eberstadt & Sons, New York
W. S. Farish III
Federal Reserve Bank of Boston
  James T. Timberlake
The First National Bank of Boston
  John W. Calkins
First Trenton National Bank
  John B. Cole, Jr.
The Franklin Savings Bank, New York
  William P. Reuss
Free Public Library of Philadelphia
  Mrs. Carolyn W. Field
  Russell Heaney
General Electric Company
  E. J. Hile
  George F. Way
Ginn and Company
The Armand Hammer Foundation
Harper & Row, Publishers
Dallett Hemphill
Hercules Inc.
  Richard B. Douglas
  Edward L. Grant
Frank Herzog (Photographer)
William Hisgrove
Hotel DuPont, Wilmington
  J. E. Allinger
Houghton Mifflin Company
John Howell—Books, San Francisco
Jay R. Huckabee
Mr. and Mrs. Peter Hurd
Curtis M. Hutchins
International Harvester Company
  of America, Inc.

J. H. Aeschliman
Interwoven, Division of Kayser-Roth
  Corporation
Randolph C. Bramwell
Iowa State University
  Dr. W. Robert Parks, President
David Jones
Mr. and Mrs. Anton Kamp
Kellogg Company
  A. J. Finley
Kennedy Galleries, Inc., New York
  Eugene Coulon
  Rudolph Wunderlich
Kirk in the Hills, Bloomfield Hills,
  Michigan
  Ralph L. Tweedale
Joseph Klemik (Photographer)
Gerald Kraus (Photographer)
Frank Lerner (Photographer)
Mr. and Mrs. Joseph E. Levine
The Library of Congress
  Dudley B. Ball
Little, Brown and Company
M. Knoedler & Co., Inc., New York
  Bernard Danenberg
John Denys McCoy
David McKay Company, Inc.
C. T. McLaughlin
Chester Marron
Metropolitan Life Insurance Company
  The late C. L. Christiernin
  Paul Mulcahy
The Minneapolis Institute of Arts
  Samuel Sachs II, Curator
Missouri State Museum, Jefferson City
  Donald M. Johnson
John Morrell & Company
  W. F. Anderson
  A. M. Johnson
Dr. and Mrs. William A. Morton, Jr.
Paul D. Myers
Nabisco, Inc.
  Miss Mary Hoban

National Cowboy Hall of Fame and
  Western Heritage Center
  Dean Krakel
*National Geographic Magazine*
  Dr. Melvin M. Payne
  Andrew Poggenpohl
Needham Free Public Library
  Mrs. Vivian McIver
The New Britain Museum of
  American Art
  Mrs. Irving Blomstrann
New York Life Insurance Company
  George H. Kelley
The New York Public Library
  Edwin S. Holmgren
  Joseph T. Rankin
The North Carolina Museum of Art
  Benjamin F. Williams, Curator
Oneida Historical Society and
  The Munson-Williams-Proctor
  Institute, Utica, New York
  Jason L. Cox
Penn Central Transportation Company
  Ralph F. Timbers
Penn Mutual Life Insurance Company
  Wilbur S. Benjamin
Pennsylvania Academy of the Fine Arts,
  Philadelphia
  Mrs. Elizabeth Bailey
Mr. and Mrs. Edward H. Porter, Jr.
Carl D. Pratt
Princeton University Library
  Alexander P. Clark
Quaker Oats Company
  Miss Lucille Nitzburg
The Reading Public Museum and
  Art Gallery, Reading
  James M. K. Waldron
W. C. Roberts
William R. Rollins
Roosevelt Hotel, New York City
  Joseph W. McCarthy
Donald P. Ross

B. F. Schlimme
Frank E. Schoonover
John Schoonover
Courtlandt Schoonover
Charles Scribner's Sons
  Charles Scribner, Jr.
Joseph E. Seagram & Sons, Inc.
Silver Burdett Company
  Mrs. Pauline Coburn
Mr. and Mrs. William V. Sipple, Jr.
C. R. Smith
Mrs. Arthur L. Smythe
Mrs. Andrew J. Sordoni, Jr.
Southern Arizona Bank & Trust
  Company, Tucson
  A. L. Ruiz
St. Andrew's School, Middletown,
  Delaware
  Dr. Robert A. Moss
  Dr. Walden Pell II
State of Missouri, Division of Commerce
  and Industrial Development
  Gerald R. Massie
Steinway & Sons, New York
  John H. Steinway
Syracuse China Corporation
  George E. Springs
Thomas Gilcrease Institute of American
  History and Art, Tulsa, Oklahoma
  Mrs. Mary Elizabeth Good
Traymore Hotel, Atlantic City
  Carroll Knauer
Alexander Ferguson Treadwell
The United Educators, Inc., Lake Bluff,
  Illinois
  Everett Edgar Sentman
United States Naval Academy,
  The Museum
  Captain A. J. Ellis, U.S.N.
University of Arizona, Museum of Art,
  Tucson
  William E. Steadman
University of South Dakota, Vermillion

Dr. Richard L. Bowen, President
U.S. Naval Ordnance Laboratory,
  Silver Spring, Maryland
  Frank Nichter
Valley National Bank, Phoenix, Arizona
  Mrs. Vera Costello
Washington Cathedral, Mount Saint
  Alban, Washington, D.C.
  John H. Bayless
Charles Waterhouse
Jack Webb
Westtown School, Westtown, Pa.
  Miss Margaret Axson
  Earl Harrison
Mr. and Mrs. George A. Weymouth
Mr. Donald Widdoes (Photographer)
William A. Farnsworth Library Art
  Museum, Rockland, Maine
  Wendell S. Hadlock, Director
William Penn Memorial Museum
  Harrisburg
  Mrs. Patricia Nemser
Wilmington Institute and New Castle
  County Libraries
Wilmington Savings Fund Society
  Mrs. Frances D. Naczi
Wilmington Trust Company
  H. Franklin Baker
Winchester-Western and The Gun
  Museum, New Haven, Conn.
  T. E. Hall
Mrs. Norman B. Woolworth
R. Frederick Woolworth
Zeal Wright (Photographer)
James B. Wyeth
Nicholas Wyeth
Mrs. Stimson Wyeth
Yale University Library
  Mrs. Joyce B. Schneider
YMCA of Wilmington and
  New Castle County

# Notes

## Chapter 1—Howard Pyle's World of Illustration

1. Charles D. Abbott, *Howard Pyle: A Chronicle* (New York: Harper & Brothers, 1925), p. 205
2. Homer Saint-Gaudens, *The American Artist and His Times* (New York: Dodd, Mead, 1941), p. 163.
3. "Circular of The School of Illustration" (Philadelphia: Drexel Institute of Art, Science and Industry, 1896/1897), p. 3.
4. Abbott, *Howard Pyle*, pp. 213–14.
5. Richard Wayne Lykes, "Howard Pyle: Teacher of Illustration" (Diss. University of Pennsylvania, 1947), p. 28.

## Chapter 2—Wyeth's Student Years

1. Joseph F. Dinneen, "Wyeth: Noted Illustrator," *Boston Sunday Globe* [n.d.].
2. Muriel Caswall, "King of the Pirates," *Boston Sunday Post* (Nov. 27, 1921).
3. From a speech by Anton Kamp, July 1951.
4. N. C. Wyeth, "For Better Illustration," *Scribner's Magazine* (Nov. 1919): 638–42.
5. N. C. Wyeth, "Pupils of Pyle Tell of His Teaching," *Christian Science Monitor* (Nov. 13, 1912).
6. Ibid.
7. Speech, Anton Kamp.
8. Wyeth, "Pupils of Pyle."
9. Ibid.
10. Sidney M. Chase, "Pupils of Wyeth Tell of His Teaching," *Christian Science Monitor* (Nov. 13, 1912).
11. N. C. Wyeth, "Howard Pyle as I Knew Him," *Mentor Magazine* (July 1927): 15–17.
12. Wyeth, "Pupils of Pyle."
13. Isabel Hoopes, "N. C. Wyeth," *All-Arts Magazine* (Sept. 1925).
14. Wyeth, "Pupils of Pyle."
15. Ibid.

## Chapter 3—N.C.'s West

1. A week after Remington's death Wyeth said, during an interview:

   "I have often considered Remington as not so much a painter as a historian. He has recorded the western life conscientiously and truthfully. Remington has always been concerned with the detail and action rather than the bigger spirit of the west, and his work will always last because it is a faithful pictorial account of a life that is fast disappearing.
   "The very fact of Remington's fidelity and photographic truthfulness has always had a great influence on all illustrators taking up the western life. This influence has no doubt had its effect on some of the local artists, though not to an extent that would be noticeable in their work.
   "Remington has been highly respected by all men of the artistic world because of his sincerity, even though he never has reached a real pinnacle in his painting."
   *The Star*, Wilmington, Del., Jan. 2, 1910

2. *The Star*, Wilmington, Del., Jan. 23, 1910.
3. Muriel Caswall, "King of the Pirates," *Boston Sunday Post* (Nov. 27, 1921).

## Chapter 5—Brandywine Country

1. "Wilmington's Colony of Artists—No. 12, N. C. Wyeth," *The Star*, Wilmington, Del., Jan. 23, 1910.
2. *Ladies' Home Journal*, July 1925.

## Chapter 6—Religious Painting

1. Isabel Hoopes, "N. C. Wyeth," *All-Arts* (Sept. 1925), p. 7.
2. "The Parables of Jesus" (An Announcement) (Boston: Unitarian Laymen's League, Dec. 25, 1923).

## Chapter 7—The Classics

1. Joseph F. Dinneen, "Wyeth, Noted Illustrator," *Boston Sunday Globe* Magazine [n.d.]
2. Letter, undated, Scribner Archive, Princeton University Library, Princeton, N.J.
3. "Book News," *Scribner's Magazine* (Dec. 1918): 12.
4. Letter, undated, Scribner Archive, Princeton University Library, Princeton, N.J.
5. Ibid.
6. Letter dated November 13, 1919, Scribner Archive, Princeton University Library, Princeton, N.J.
7. Ibid.
8. Letter, undated, Scribner Archive, Princeton University Library, Princeton, N.J.
9. Letter dated June 14, 1920, Scribner Archive, Princeton University Library, Princeton, N.J.
10. Letter dated July 19, 1920, Scribner Archive, Princeton University Library, Princeton, N.J.
11. N. C. Wyeth, Preface to *Robinson Crusoe*.
12. Letter dated July 19, 1920, Scribner Archive, Princeton University Library, Princeton, N.J.
13. Letter dated August 17, 1921, Scribner Archive, Princeton University Library, Princeton, N.J.
14. Letter dated August 21, 1921, Scribner Archive, Princeton University Library, Princeton, N.J.
15. Letter dated June 20, 1929, Scribner Archive, Princeton University Library, Princeton, N.J.
16. Letter dated June 25, 1929, Scribner Archive, Princeton University Library, Princeton, N.J.
17. Letter dated August 19, 1929, Scribner Archive, Princeton University Library, Princeton, N.J.
18. Marjorie Kinnan Rawlings, *The Yearling* (New York: Charles Scribner's Sons, 1929). Excerpt from the Wyeth letter was reproduced in the limited edition only.

## Chapter 8—From Blackbeard to St. Nick

1. N. C. Wyeth, "On Illustration—A Suggestion and a Comment on Illustrating Fiction," *The New York Times* (Oct. 13, 1912): 574.
2. *The Ladies' Home Journal* (July 1925).
3. The Scribner Archive, Princeton University Library, Princeton, N.J.
4. *A Book of Notable American Illustrators*, Walker Engraving Company, N.Y., 1927

## Chapter 9—Commercial Art

1. The Scribner Archive, Princeton University Library, Princeton, N.J.

## Chapter 10—Murals, Lunettes, and the Triptych

1. Letter, undated, Scribner Archive, Princeton University Library, Princeton, N.J.
2. "Mural Paintings in the First National Bank of Boston," *The Ladies' Home Journal* (July 1925).
3. Letter, undated, Scribner Archive, Princeton University Library, Princeton, N.J.
4. "N. C. Wyeth Mural," *Delaware Today* (Feb.-March 1967).
5. Information on St. Andrew's School and its mural was furnished in correspondence with the Reverend Walker Pell II, first headmaster of the school.
6. "The Days of the Pilgrims Live Again," *The Home Office* (employee paper of the Metropolitan Life Insurance Company) (Dec. 1941).

## Chapter 11—Easel Painting

1. Ernest W. Watson, "N. C. Wyeth, Giant on a Hilltop," *American Artist* (Jan. 1945).
2. Ibid.
3. N. C. Wyeth, "For Better Illustration," *Scribner's Magazine* (Nov. 1919).
4. Harvey Dunn, "An Evening in the Classroom," Privately printed pamphlet, 1934.
5. Letter (circa 1921) to Joseph Chapin, Scribner Archive, Princeton University Library, Princeton, N.J.
6. Letter, undated, to Joseph Chapin, Scribner Archive, Princeton University Library, Princeton, N.J.
7. Isabel Hoopes, "N. C. Wyeth," *All-Arts* (Sept. 1925).
8. Letter dated June 20, 1929, to Joseph Chapin, Scribner Archive, Princeton University Library, Princeton, N.J.

# Index

Italic page numbers indicate illustrations.

## A

Abbey, Edwin A., 125
Above the Sea of Round, Shiny Backs the Thin Loops Swirled, 38
Admirable Outlaw, The, 37
Alaska, 143, 143
Alchemist, The, 153
Allons! . . . It Is Time to Make an End, 140
Almighty Exciting Race, An, 34
"America in the Making," 156
American Flag, The, 156
American Legion Magazine, 156
And Lawless, Keeping Half a Step in Front of His Companion . . . Studied Out Their Path, 88
And When They Came to the Sword the Hand Held, King Arthur Took It Up . . . , 100
Ann Stuyvesant, 175
Apotheosis of the Family, The, 165, 170–71
Apotheosis of Franklin, An, 161, 161
Arthurs, Stanley, 21, 31
Arundel, 123
As Broadwell Raced West, 26
Ashley, Clifford, 23
Astrologer, The, 79
At the World's Fair in '93, 144
Aunt Jemina Campaign, 143, 145
Autumn, 61, 157

## B

Balfour of the House of Shaws, 85
Ball . . . Rolled Straight Toward the Goal, The, 31
Battle, The, 128
Battle at Glens Falls, The, 98
Battle of Stirling Castle, The, 96
Battle of Westport, The, 158
Battle of Wilson's Creek, 158
Bayless, John H., 167
Bear Hunters, The, 144
Beethoven and Nature, 145, 148
Ben Gunn, 86
Beth Norvell, 42
Betts, Ethel Franklin, 21
Beyond Uncharted Seas Columbus Finds a New World, 169
Big Black Beppo and Little Black Beppo, 137
Billy the Kid and Bob Ollinger, 42
Black Arrow, The, 84, 114
Black Arrow Flieth Nevermore, The, 91
Boston Blackie Forced Drawer After Drawer, 129
Boy Christ in the Carpenter's Shop, The, 73
Boy Columbus on the Wharf in Genoa, The, 136
Boy's King Arthur, The, 85, 114
Boys of St. Timothy's, 31
Bringing Home the Pumpkins, 70
Bronco Buster, 26, 26, 27, 27, 144
Bucking, 40
Buffalo Hunt, 117
Building the First White House, 148, 151
Buttonwood Farm, 179, 182

## C

Calendar illustrations, 143, 146, 147, 147, 152, 153, 153, 155, 156, 156
California Mission, A, 136
Calling the Sun Dance, 52
Canada Geese in Fall, 168
Cannibal Shore, 179
Captain Bill Bones, 78
Captain Bones Routs Black Dog, 80
Captain Nemo, 92
Carpetbaggers, The, 131
Carvers of the Sphinx, The, 147, 152
Century magazine, 33
Chapel of the Holy Spirit at the Washington Cathedral: triptych in, 77, 167–68, 172
Chapin, Joseph, 99, 128, 141, 159
Charles Scribner's Sons. See Scribner Illustrated Classics
Cherished Memory, A, 154, 156
Child, The, 72
Children of the Bible, 77
Christmas cards: paintings of parables used as, 77
Christmas Day, 142, 145
Christmas in Old Virginia, 147
Christmas Ship in Old New York, The, 147, 149
Cimarron, 53
Classics, the: illustrations for, 78–121
Collier's Weekly, 30, 31, 34
Columbian Magazine, 163
Columbus' Landing, 136
Come Live With Us, For I Think Thou Art Chosen, 72
Coming of the Mayflower, The, 169
Commercial art, 141–56
Aunt Jemina Mills, 143, 145
bank holiday posters, 142, 145
Berwind-White Coal Mining Company, 147
Blue Buckle OverAlls, 143, 144
Brown & Bigelow, 153, 156
calendar illustrations, 143, 146, 147, 147, 152, 153, 153, 155, 156, 156
Coca-Cola, 153
Cream of Wheat paintings, 141, 143
Fisk Tire, 143
Frankfort Distilleries, 152–53
General Electric Company, 152
Hercules Incorporated, 153
International Harvester Company, 152
Interwoven Stocking Company, 147
John Morrell & Company, 153, 156
Lucky Strike cigarettes, 152
New York Life Insurance, 153
patriotic posters, 147–48, 150–51
Pennsylvania Railroad, 147–48
Pierce-Arrow, 143
Steinway & Sons, 145, 147
W. K. Kellogg Company, 143
Winchester Arms, 141, 143
Confederate Battle Flag—Faithful Troops Cheer General Lee, The, 155

Corn Harvest, 184
Corn Harvest on the Brandywine, 180
Corn Harvest in the Hill Country, 70
Cornhusker, The, 156
Cosmopolitan Book Corporation, 85, 92, 114, 118
Cosmopolitan magazine, 33
Country Gentleman, 71
Courtship of Miles Standish, The, 85, 95, 118
Cover illustrations, 27, 65, 68, 71, 136
Crows in Winter, 168
Custer's Last Stand, 152, 152
Cutting Out, 41

## D

Dark and Bloody Ground, The, 152
Dark Harbor Fisherman, 186, 191
David Balfour, 84, 118
David McKay, Publisher, 85, 96, 114, 118
Davis, Charles, H., 23
"Day with the Round-Up, A," 35, 38–43
Death of Finnward Keelfarer, The, 133
Deep Cove Lobsterman, 182
Deerslayer, The, 118
Deerslayer Threw All His Force, 120
Delineator, The, 31
Departure of the Mayflower, The, 169
Die Walküre—The Magic Fire Spell, 145
Discoverer, The, 164–65
Discovery of the Chest, The, 121
Dobbin, 67
Dr. Clapton, 192
Doryman, The, 185
Drexel Institute of Art, Science and Industry: Howard Pyle's courses at, 19–21, 125
Drifts Became Heavier, The, 127
Driving the Cattle Where the Meadow Brook Is Brawling, 63
Drums, 121
Duel, The, 115
Dust wrapper illustrations, 123

## E

Egrets in Summer, 168
Eight Miners Followed the Treacherous Trail, The, 126
Emerging Into an Opening . . . , 117
Engle, William Clothier, 160
Eric Pape School of Art, 23
Eseldorf Was a Paradise for Us Boys, 94
Exhibition of Self-Effacement, An, 29

## F

Federal Reserve Bank of Boston: murals for, 159, 163
Fence Builders, 176, 179
Fight in the Forest, The, 105
Fight with Old Slewfoot, 119

Fight in the Peaks, The, 134
Fight on the Plains, A, 54
Fighting the Fire from the Telephone Poles, 29
First Aid to the Hungry, 141, 143
First Cargo, The, 124
First Farmer of the Land, 139
First Harvest, 169
First Kentucky Derby, The, 152, 153
First Mechanics National Bank of Trenton: mural for, 163-65, 171
First National Bank of Boston: murals for, 160, 166
"Flags in American History," 156
Flight Across the Lake, The, 15
. . . Flung the Six Pounds of Powerful Explosive Out Into the Great Snow Comb, 126
Fort Dearborn Massacre, The, 152
Founders of Our National Policies, The, 163
Fourth of July, 142, 145
Francisco Vasquez de Coronado, 156
Franklin, Benjamin, 161
Franklin Savings Bank (N.Y.C.): mural for, 161, 161
From an Upper Snow Platform . . . a Second Man Heaved Them Over the Bank, 126
Frontier Trapper, 134
Frontiersman, The, 128
Frost, A. B., 125

## G

Galleons, The, 157
General Washington's Entrance Into Trenton, 163-65, 171
Giant, The, 18, 160
Going to Church, 169
Golden Age of American Illustration, 125, 127–28
Golyer, 129
Good Housekeeping magazine, 77
Green, Elizabeth Shippen, 20
Gulliver's Travels, 99, 102, 106

## H

Hahn Pulled His Gun and Shot Him Through the Middle, 35
Half Moon in the Hudson, 160, 167
Hands Up, 36
Harding, George, 24
Harper & Brothers Publishers, 85, 114
Harper's Monthly, 33
Harper's Weekly, 33
He Rode Away, Following a Dim Trail, 48
He Was . . . Surprised at the Singularity of the Stranger's Appearance, 106
Headpiece illustration, 129
He'd Let a Roar Outer Him, an' Mebbe He'd Sing, "Hail Columbia, Happy Land!", 132
Hiawatha's Fishing, 59
Homer, Winslow, 125, 179
Hostage, The, 83
Hotel Roosevelt (N.Y.C.): triptych for, 160, 167
Hotel Utica

murals for, 58, 157, 159, *160*
tableware for, 159, *159*
Houghton Mifflin Company, 85, 99, 118, 121
Howard Pyle School of Art, 24–26, 28–30
N. C. Wyeth attending, 24–31
*Howard Pyle's Studio,* 23
Hoyt, Philip, 21
*Hungry, But Stern on the Depot Platform,* 43
*Hunter, The,* 56
*Hupper Farm, The, 181*
Hurd, Peter, 189

**I**

*I Hereby Pronounce Yuh Man and Wife!,* 37
*I Saw His Horse Jump Back Dodgin' a Rattlesnake or Somethin',* 35
*I Stood Like One Thunderstruck . . . , 109*
*I would like to have known my grandfather better,* 153
*In the Crystal Depths,* 60
*In the Dark Days of the Civil War, 163*
*In a Dream I Meet General Washington,* 165
*In Old Kentucky,* 148, *150*
*In Penobscot Bay, 187,* 191
Indian, Woodland. *See* Woodland Indian
*Indian Fisherman, The,* 157, *160*
*Indian Hunter, The,* 157, *160*
*Into Town from the South,* 26
*Invocation to the Buffalo Herds,* 53
*Island Funeral, 182,* 189
*I've Sold Them Wheelers,* 54

**J**

J. Walter Thompson Company, 143
*Jim Bludsoe of the Prairie Belle, 131*
*Jim Hawkins Leaves Home,* 84
*Jinglebob,* 121
*John Oxenham, 108*

**K**

*Kidnapped, 84,* 114
*King Edward, 110*
*King Mark Slew the Noble Knight Sir Tristram, 104*
*King's Henchman, The,* 145

**L**

*Ladies' Home Journal,* 161, 184, 186
*Langford of the Three Bars,* 42
*Last of the Chestnuts, 177*
*Last of the Mohicans, The,* 89, 114
*Last Stand, The,* 36
*Lee of the Grub-Wagon, The,* 38
*Legends of Charlemagne,* 118
*Leslie's Popular Monthly,* 28, 30
*Letters of a Woman Homesteader,* 53
*Lift Up Your Hearts,* 156
*Listen to What I'm Tellin' Ye!,* 35
Little, Brown & Company, 121
*Little Breeches, 129*
*Little Shepherd of Kingdom Come, The, 106,* 121
*Lively Lady, The,* 123
*Lobstering Off Black Spruce Ledge, 183,* 191
*Lobsterman, The, 183*
*Long Henry Drove Cautiously Across the Scene of Yesterday's Accident, 126*
*Long John Silver and Hawkins, 10*

*Lost Lamb, The,* 77
*Lumber, 155*
Lunettes. *See also* Murals
for Missouri state capital, *158,* 159

**M**

*Magic Pool, The,* 57
*Maine Sea Captain's Daughter, A, 175*
*Man With a Pistol,* 25
*Map of Discovery—Eastern Hemisphere, 170*
McBurney, James, 21
*McClure's Magazine,* 42
McCouch, Gordon, 24
McCoy, John, 171
*Melissa, 118*
*Men Against the Sea,* 125
Metropolitan Life Insurance Company: murals for, *168,* 169 171, *172*
*Metropolitan* magazine, 30
*Mexican Shepherd, 50*
*Michael Strogoff,* 121
*Midnight Encounter, The, 114*
*Minute Men, The,* 30, *30,* 31
Missouri state capitol: lunettes for, *158,* 159
*Mrs. Cushman's House, 186,* 191
"*Moods, The,*" 58, *61,* 157
*Moose Call, The,* 58, *58*
*Moose Hunters, The,* 143
*Moose Hunters—A Moonlit Night, 125*
*Mowing,* 64, 65
*Muhammad the Prophet,* 74
Murals, 157–72. *See also* Lunettes; Triptychs
Federal Reserve Bank of Boston, 159, *163*
First Mechanics National Bank of Trenton, 163–65, *171*
First National Bank of Boston, 160, *166*
Franklin Savings Bank (N.Y.C.), 161, *161*
Hotel Roosevelt (N.Y.C.), 160–61, *167*
*Hotel Utica,* 58, 157, 159, *160*
Metropolitan Life Insurance Company, 168, 169, 171, 172
National Geographic Society headquarters, 161–62, *164–65, 169, 170*
Penn Mutual Life Insurance Company, 166–67
Traymore Hotel (Atlantic City), 159, *162*
Westtown School of Westtown, Pa., *18,* 160
Wilmington Savings Fund Society, 165–66, *170*
Pilgrim series, 169, 171–72
St. Andrew's School (Middletown, Del.), 168–69
*Mutiny on the Bounty,* 125
*Mysterious Island, The,* 85–86, 114
*Mysterious Stranger, The,* 85, 114
*Mystery Tree, The,* 55

**N**

*'N There's a Dragon Black as Ink wi' One Eye, 132*
*Nan of Music Mountain,* 53
National Geographic Society headquarters: murals for, 161–62, *164–65, 169, 170*
*Nativity, The, 75*
*Navajo Herder in the Foothills,* 45
Navajo studies, 32
*Near Them Was Standing an Indian, in Attitude Stern and Defiant, 102*

*New Trails,* 153
*New World, A,* 153
*New Year's Day, 142,* 145
*Newborn Calf, 178,* 182
*Night Herder, A,* 41
*Nightfall, 189,* 191
Nixon, Richard M., 148
*Nothing Would Escape Them,* 49
*Now, Major, for the best part of the game,* 153
Noyes, George, 159

**O**

Oakley, Thornton, 24
*Odyssey of Homer, The,* 99, 121
*Oh, Morgan's Men Are Out for You; and Blackbeard— Buccaneer!, 133*
*Old Pew,* 81
*Ole St. Nick, 135*
*On the Island of Erraid,* 87
*Opium Smoker, The, 131*
*Ore Wagon, The,* 54
*Oregon Trail, The,* 53, 121
*Outing Magazine, The,* 33, 42, 43, 58

**P**

*Parable of the Leaven, The,* 72
*Parable of the Net, The,* 76, *76*
*Parable of the Seed, The,* 76, *76*
*Parables of Jesus,* 72, *73,* 76, *76*
paintings of, used as Christmas cards, 77
*Parables of Jesus, The,* 77
*Parkman Outfit, The—Henry Chatillon, Guide and Hunter, 116*
Parrish, Maxfield, 20
*Partnership for the Sake of Greater Safety, A,* 43
*Pastoral of the South-West,* 51
Patriotic posters, 147–48, *150–51*
*Paul Revere, 111*
*Pay Stage, The,* 44
Peck, Henry, 23
"*Peculiarsome*" *Abe, 138*
Pen-and-ink drawings
for "Back to the Farm," 62
for *Susanna and Sue,* 69, 71
Penn Mutual Life Insurance Company: mural for, 166–67
*Pennsylvania Farmer, 190,* 191
preliminary study for, *190*
*Peter Minuit, 174*
*Phoenician Biremes, The, 166*
Pilgrim murals, 169, 171, 172
*Pioneers, The,* 153
*Pitcairn's Island,* 125
*Pittsburgh in the Beginning—Fort Prince George,* 148, *151*
*Plains Herder, The,* 47
*Poems of American Patriotism,* 89, 118
*Popular Magazine, The,* 71
*Preparing for the Mutiny,* 82
*Primal Chemistry,* 153
*Primitive Spearman, A,* 58, *61*
*Priscilla and John Alden,* 169
*Progressive Farmer,* 71
*Prospector, The,* 36
*Public Test of the World's First Reaper,* 149, *152*
Pyle, Howard, 19, *19,* 20–21, 24–25, 29–30, 63, 65, 125, 127, 138, 173
courses of, at the Drexel Institute of Art, Science and Industry, 19–21, 125
formation of school in Wilmington, Delaware, 21, 125. *See also* Howard Pyle School of Art
studio of, *23*
with a group of his students, *24, 25*

**R**

*Rabble in Arms,* 123
*Racing for Dinner,* 37
*Ramona,* 53, 114, 121
Reed, Charles W., 23, 174
Religious painting, 72–77
Remington, Frederic, 33–34, 125
*Reminiscences of a Ranchman,* 53
*Return of the Hunter, The,* 159, *160*
reproduced on tableware, 159, *159*
*Returning Soldier, The,* 156
*Ringing Out Liberty,* 148, *150*
*Rip Van Winkle,* 41, 85, 96, *112,* 118
*Road to the Jones House, The, 187*
*Road to Vidalia, The, 122*
*Robin and His Mother Go to Nottingham Fair,* 92
*Robin Hood,* 85, 114
*Robin Hood and His Companions Lend Aid . . . from Ambush,* 97
*Robin Hood and the Men of the Greenwood,* 95
*Robin Meets Maid Marian, 101*
*Robinson Crusoe,* 85, 92, 95, 96, 114
*Romance of Adventure,* 6
"*Romance of Commerce, The,*" 156
*Roping Horses in the Corral,* 33
*Rounding-Up,* 40

**S**

St. Andrew's School (Middletown, Del.): mural in, 168–69
*Sam Houston,* 153
*Saturday Evening Post, The,* 27, 30, 31, 42, 133
Schoonover, Frank E., 21, *31*
*Scottish Chiefs, The,* 96, 118
Scribner Illustrated Classics, 79–80, 84, 85–86, 89, 92, 95–96, 99, 102, 110, 114, 118, 121, 173
*Scribner's Magazine,* 30, 31, 33, 34–35, 38 n., 42, 43, 45 n., 58, 65, 73, 157
*Scythers, The,* 66
*Sea Wolf, The,* 152
*Seeker, The,* 153
Segantini, Giovanni, 182
Self-portraits
(circa 1896), 22
(1900), 22
(1913), 2
*September Afternoon, 173,* 182
*She Makes a Grand Light, 139*
"*Sheep-Herder of the South-West, A,*" 43, 45–51
*Siege of the Round-House, The,* 90
*Silent Burial, The,* 60
*Silent Fisherman, The,* 58, 59
*Sir Mador's Spear Brake All to Pieces But the Other's Spear Held,* 93
*Sir Nigel Sustains England's Honor in the Lists, 113*
*Sitting Up Cross-Legged, With Each Hand Holding a Gun,* 54
Sloan, John, 179
Smith, Jessie Wilcox, 20
*Soldiers of the Soil,* 156
"Solitude" series, 57, 58, *58,* 59, *60*
advertisement for portfolio of, 59
preliminary study for, 58
*Song of the Eagle That Mates With the Storm, 133*
*Sounding Sea, 179*
*Spearman, The,* 60

*Spirit of '46, The,* 153
*Spring,* 61
*Spring House, The,* 188, *191*
*Still Life With Iris and Oranges,*
*180*
*Still Life With Apples,* 175
*Still Life With Brush,* 176
Stillwell, Sarah, 21
*Stonewall Jackson,* 130
*Success* magazine, 28, 30
*Summer,* 61, 157
*Summer Days,* 177
*Summer Night,* 174, *181,* 191
*Sun Glint,* 182
*Susanna and Sue,* 71
*Sweet Land of Liberty,* 153

**T**

*Thanksgiving Day, 142,* 145
*Thanksgiving Feast, The,* 169
*There Was an Old Woman Tost*
*Up in a Basket,* 137
*These Folks Were Evidently*
*Amusing Themselves . . . ,*
*107*
Thompson, Ellen, 21
*Throwback, The,* 42
*Toby, fetch me the key to the*
*springhouse,* 153
*Torch Race, The, 147,* 152
*. . . Trading from the Battle-*
*mented Walls . . . , 30*

*Traymore Hotel* (Atlantic City):
murals for, 159, *162*
*Treasure Island,* 79–80, 84, 114
*Trending into Maine,* 123
Triptychs
in Chapel of the Holy Spirit at
the Washington Cathedral, 77,
167–68, *172*
in Hotel Roosevelt (N.Y.C.),
160–61, *167*
True, Allen, *24*
*Turkey Hunt, The,* 169
"Twelve Artists Depict America,"
156
*Twenty Thousand Leagues Under*
*the Sea,* 86
*Two Boys in a Punt,* 71
*Two Surveyors, 28*

**U**

*Union Troops Boarding Missis-*
*sippi Steamers,* 140
Unitarian Laymen's League, 73

**V**

*Vandemark's Folly,* 53
*Vedette, The,* 127

**W**

*Wagner and Liszt, 145, 145*
*War Clouds, The,* 55

*War Whoop, The,* 152
*Water-Hole, The, 114*
*We Joined the Second Expedition,*
*34*
*We Must Be in the Dungeon . . . ,*
*89*
*Wedding Procession, The,* 169
West, the, 31–56
"Day with the Round-Up, A,"
35, *38–43*
"Sheep-Herder of the South-
West," 43, *45–51*
*Westward Ho!,* 89, 92, 95, 114
*When He Comes He Will Rule*
*Over the Whole World, 72*
*Where the Mail Goes Cream of*
*Wheat Goes,* 144
*Whispering Smith, 42*
*White Company, The,* 85, 118
*Why Don't You Speak for*
*Yourself, John?, 103*
*William Penn, Man of Courage—*
*Vision—Action,* 166–67
Wilmington Savings Fund Society:
mural for, 165–66, *170*
*Woman's Home Companion,* 53
*Woodland Indian, the,* 56–61
"Moods, The," 58, *61,* 157
"Solitude" series, 57, 58, *58,*
*59, 60*
Wyeth, Andrew, 171
Wyeth, Newell Convers, 24, *31,*
65, 68, *190,* 191

attending the Eric Pape School
of Art, 23
attending the Howard Pyle
School of Art, 24–31
childhood of, 22–23
death of, 171
elected to the National Academy, 191
exterior and interior views of
studio of, *84*
in costume of Little John at
Howard Pyle Studio, *29*
marriage of, 63
out West, 31–56. *See also*
West, the
posed with illustrations, *132*
self-portraits of. *See* Self-
portraits
settling in Chadds Ford, Pennsylvania, 63, 68
as stickler for historic accuracy, 163
views of, about magazine illustration, 128, 130, 133
at work on a mural, *157*
Wyeth, Mrs. Newell Convers
(Carolyn B. Bockius), 63

**Y**

*Yearling, The,* 110, 121
Young, James Webb, 143
*Youth's Companion,* 33